The Essential Code

Feeling the Urgency of Your Heart

Arvetta M Souza

BALBOA.
PRESS

A DIVISION OF HAY HOUSE

Balboa Press books may be ordered through booksellers or by contacting:

Balboa Press
A Division of Hay House
1663 Liberty Drive
Bloomington, IN 47403
www.balboapress.com
1-(877) 407-4847

ISBN: 978-1-4525-4431-1 (sc)
ISBN: 978-1-4525-4433-5 (hc)
ISBN: 978-1-4525-4432-8 (e)

Library of Congress Control Number: 2011963146

Because of the dynamic nature of the Internet, any web addresses or
links contained in this book may have changed since publication and
may no longer be valid. The views expressed in this work are solely those
of the author and do not necessarily reflect the views of the publisher,
and the publisher hereby disclaims any responsibility for them.

The author of this book does not dispense medical advice or prescribe the use
of any technique as a form of treatment for physical, emotional, or medical
problems without the advice of a physician, either directly or indirectly. The
intent of the author is only to offer information of a general nature to help
you in your quest for emotional and spiritual well-being. In the event you use
any of the information in this book for yourself, which is your constitutional
right, the author and the publisher assume no responsibility for your actions.

Any people depicted in stock imagery provided by Thinkstock are
models, and such images are being used for illustrative purposes only.
Certain stock imagery © Thinkstock.

Printed in the United States of America

Balboa Press rev. date: 2/23/2012

I extend boundless gratitude to every beautiful soul who has touched my life, knowingly, and unknowingly; for the lessons you taught me, the joys we shared, and for the events that inspired me to study, to learn, to understand more deeply. I will forever be grateful to all who participated in elevating my spiritual being. Michael, my heart returns your deep love; my deepest gratitude for awaking me from worldly illusions. I treasure the mystical gift of consciousness, and knowing that life does not end, it just changes. Love and blessings forever

"Out beyond right and wrong lies a field.
Meet me there." Where
Divine Truths mesmerize the mind
and awesomeness of Spirit
illuminate the soul.

QUOTATION: POET, RUMI—ADDED PHRASE: ARVETTA SOUZA

"The universe is illumined by a spiritual intelligence that goes beyond description. It is this exact ability that makes itself known to every cell within all life forms. And so it is that I am the spirit, grace, and action of this knowledge as the human connection."

—REVEREND ANGELA PEREGOFF

CONTENTS

I extend my deepest gratitude to
artist Daniel Holeman
for his beautiful book cover,
the "Cosmic Consciousness" art
at the end of this book,
and for his talented Web design
for "The Essential Code" website.

Daniel's website: www.AwakenVisions.com

www.TheEssentialCode.com

INTRODUCTION

"And the time came, when the risk to remain tight in the bud was more painful than the risk it took to bloom."
—ANAIS NIN

Thomas Berry's cosmological wisdom compassionately presented humanity with a heart-based quest for the healing of our once-vibrant resource, planet Earth, *a living, breathing organism* that humanity calls home. Thomas Berry, along with quantum physicist Dr. Brian Swimme, worked passionately as dedicated teachers regarding our planet being more than a fireball encrusted with earthen dirt and seas of water or a home to be used and abused according to man's desires, pleasures, and sacrilegious benefits. Earth is a sacred creation; we stand on sacred ground. We came from its waters and the stardust of creation. An enigma of our creation: we are a part of the earth; what we do to the earth, we do to ourselves.

More than forty years ago, Thomas Berry, Geologist, informed earth's inhabitants about the ill state of our planet and the consequences of our continued use and abuse, as if it were a tool. What do we do with tools? We use and abuse them and then toss them aside when no longer useful. Instead of becoming conscious and caring, the majority of humanity not only continued their abusive patterns, but our insatiable habits proliferated.

Today, man is waking up to what he has done, not only to the earth but to ourselves. As Chief Seattle stated, "Man belongs to the earth, the earth does not belong to us." We are made of the same chemicals present in the earth, the rocks, plants, and stars! We truly are part of creation. To effectively heal the earth, man first has to know who he truly is and to *heal himself.* The condition of the earth and our environment is like a mirror of mankind. **Humanity healing is a mirror for the ages**—only through healing of our "false self" can we be truly spiritual people, individually and collectively, to blossom into our true and magnificent *spirit-selves.*

Only through growth in one's spiritual self does one elevate his or her frequency level, vibrating a pulsating, heart-based love outward, connecting to the electromagnetic waves in the cosmos. Energies of the cosmos are of divine essence. The ***symbolic vision in humanity healing*** is that of *emerging, co-creative, universal humans, co-creating a sustainable and evolving future in communities of loving union.*

The challenge of this profoundness of being is to embed a knowing of one's spirit self. To know self is an *inward,* psychological journey. *Dogma* is of the *external* world and *comes from man's ego, not from divine source.* Dogma exerts control, laws, and denominational identity—creating separateness, versus an evolutionary, universal oneness. Not only is medieval leadership outdated, so are dogmas of the past. Religious rituals can medicate, soothe the ego, and praise our Source but will not and cannot heal and transition the psyche to one's authentic self. Instead, all too often, one will become addicted (one of man's ills in need of healing), versus finding one's true sense of self. This type of healing is a process only obtained outside of the fundamentalism found in dogma and religious rituals, unlike the profound inner levitation experience of an evolutionary consciousness.

The spirit cannot be boxed in, and neither can spiritual growth. What would the masters think of the dogmas if they were here on earth today—Christ, Buddha, and all the others who are transcended souls of a universal and loving presence? There is a time for all things! The evolutionary path of humanity is a constant, changing, growing process. The path to evolutionary consciousness demands "stepping out of line" from the norm (the repetitive and mundane lifestyle of common, shared beliefs and rituals). The profound incubates and evolves out of the mundane to a deep and illuminating divinity. Spontaneous healing of beliefs is **not an end to our world**; neither is the end of the Mayan calendar. They are **just an end to our illusions** and the path to advancing one's soul to an illuminating destiny. The choice is ours.

The choice is urgent; the old world and its ways are breaking down. The divine energies of the new world age sustain the sacred synergies, as presented in the *"Essential Code."*

Our choice is the difference between the fate of humanity and a divine destiny—a "turning of the heart" to a loving energy, pulsating a synergy of sacred waves connecting with the cosmos; along with new co-creative global systems that sustain the integrity of planet Earth and humankind. These are not passive thoughts. It's urgent and vital to the preservation of Mother Earth and her various species of life, including ours! Otherwise, the question is, "Do we wish to live or fade away?" We have seen the world's chaos and destruction in a matter of minutes. Is anyone listening? Is everyone sleeping? Nature's alarm is screeching for human awakening.

> *"Sometimes that's all it takes: One person doing the seemingly impossible in the presence of others. In witnessing the limits broken, they can then hold the new possibility in their minds, because they've personally experienced it."*
> (GREGG BRADEN, THE SPONTANEOUS HEALING OF BELIEFS, HAY HOUSE 2008, 108)

This book offers narratives of educational life stories and everlasting, life-enhancing tools for gaining an

educated and informed conscience, **enabling one to let go of the limitations that bind and transcend the ego that controls. These are the preliminary steps for transformation to a new species: a universal humanity and a resonant future of community, oneness, and a joyful and balanced existence.**

Because the Catholic Church and Vatican II represent the world's largest church, it influences or dismays a large portion of our populace. Therefore, understanding its relevance in the world is an important aspect of an educated and informed conscience and the enablement of humanity healing, while merged in the changing energies of a new world age. Therefore, the church, a short measure of Vatican II, the new religion, and the state of the church today are discussed in this book as relevant to the urgent and mandatory transitions of our world today.

There are many writings and programs inspiring a deep paradigm shift to greater spiritual awareness. This shift includes transitions of the human heart—an intelligence of heart-consciousness and a destiny beyond our wildest dreams.

The *Essential Code* is our sacred heart-intelligence, centered in evolutionary consciousness. The state of being unconscious of our evolutionary journey exposes one to negative energies such as fear, separateness, stress, confusion, and feelings of helplessness. Not even the media can offer effective answers or go to the core of recessed fear, anger, and frustrations. If anything, our world seems more desolate after listening to media trivia. The pages within this book will guide you into a consciousness of your own evolutionary journey by tapping into your inner unconscious sacred code and evolve your awareness to a sacred interconnectedness through the heart.

The *Essential Code* is the incarnate sacred path. A feeling of the sacredness of being, grounded in an urgency for all humanity. There is a heartfelt concern for those in the sea of humanity who feel anger and indifference and patterns of being that are no longer sustainable in the energy waves of the fast-emerging birth of a new world age.

New cosmic energies emerge as the old world we have ingrained in our psyche dissipates. Stresses of this transition affect all areas of experience and behaviors, such as the changing weather patterns that devastate many areas of the globe. As we experience the chaos of cosmic and global change, the world and systems we have known are failing everywhere, forcing changes in attitudes, practices, systems, and lifestyles. *The years of high consumption are gone. Lost jobs will not return. New entrepreneurial challenges are arising for creating sustainable environments and co-creative communities; change is essential and constant!*

There is a silver lining behind every cloud. To be alive, here on earth today, means that we are the chosen people, the first species to consciously help birth and nurture a new cosmic embryo, the new world age. We are the chosen co-creators of history in the making—a transformation challenging mankind to reinvent themselves, while giving birth to a local and global system of co-creative coherence. Transformations tend to challenge our creative powers and our trust in life. Allowing fear to control our lives is not an option.

It is inevitable that fear and faith cannot operate in the same space and time. Faith *is* "stepping out of line"; profound growth requires stepping outside of your "comfort box." Faith keeps one moving forward with courage, strength, and openness to the new. The spirit never stands still, is constantly moving, and always supports one's stretching to a new awareness and higher frequency of being.

Connecting with the Cosmos

The unbalanced structures of today will not be sustainable in the new emerging field of cosmic energy. These energies are unfolding now; a new cosmic birth has evolved! When we try to hold on to what is ending, leaving, or changing in our lives, we are pulled kicking into the next realm. This is a much slower, painful process than letting go and flowing with the new, even when the new is ambiguous or unknown. As Scripture reveals, "the old dies as the new is born" (Corinthians 5:17 English Standard Version). I can vouch for this and the deep resonance of faith that it summons.

It's not the end of our world but an end to our illusions.

It is imperative that people self-create new dimensions of being and participate in the cosmic birthing process. Our choices will determine our destiny.

Why do feelings matter in the emergence of the new world age? Let's begin by understanding how we are connected to cosmic energy. The beating, *feeling* vibrations of our heart carry electromagnetic waves that vibrate outward and connect to the electromagnetic waves in the universe. The universe is an essence of loving, divine energy. Our loving and heart-based feelings become sacred energy, radiating the essence of our choices, and *who we are, from our hearts' inner messages!* The *Essential Code* enables one to feel the sacredness of being, to master the humanness of one's spirit, creating a new species. The species is referred to as Universal Humans, an energy that is coherent with the divine cosmic energy, the next era emerging into being, now.

The Essential Code incarnates a transcended ego with deep feelings of peace, love, forgiveness, appreciation, gratitude, and compassion. Then, bonding this indispensable essence within one's heart as one's sacred way of being and living. Swift embodiment of this sacred way of being, and co-creating new systems in community and unity, is an urgency of all time!

Do you choose fate or the destiny of your dreams? To have the kind of world we want, we have to be the kind of person we want the world to be. The *Essential Code* embodies this evolutionary, sacred path. The same higher-frequency energy is present in the emerging cosmic embryo, its cosmic birth being "Day One," December 22, 2012.

Crises throughout our global village indicate an all-inclusive urgency for the whole planetary body to quicken and embody *the Essential Code*, align with the new wisdom, and transcend old ways of being, shifting to a heart-based, co-creative society—living, working, and being in communion and unity. As Barbara Marx Hubbard stated in a visit with the Virtual Co-Creative Community, "*We are here to birth and install the code for a new Global Operating System.*" Wow! That's huge. But the methodologies are sacred simplicities! *We*—implies "Universal Humans," an emergent species incarnated in an evolutionary consciousness, actively installing new local and global systems.

In my Soul Therapy Practitioner course, I recently discovered that I am an old soul working through level seven. Meaning I am an old soul in the last stage this side of the veil. The secrets of life have become mundane. I wish to know the secrets of the evolutionary universe, to help transgress unsustainable systems and to help others advance their soul. Life circumstances have challenged me to respond in deep expressions of God's grace, due to a highly active life of ongoing intensity, at a depth intolerable by many. The circumstances of life often send me searching for knowledge and understanding. For me, yearning to understand *everything* is like a deep itch longing to be scratched.

May the content of this book inspire others into choosing to evolve. I have shared personal experiences and forever-applicable lifetime tools, based on sacred truths and universal principles, and references that sustain these truths. My hope is that, in sharing this journey of insight, it will create an educated conscience, awaken a deep and conscious journey of heart intelligence, a mastering of one's spirit, and advancement of the soul. My intent is to light a candle, kindle a fire, and open the "third eye" (to see without seeing) while embedding the *Essential Code*, and accelerating the global emergence of a new human species.

The creating Source, Universe, Higher Being, and all other references defining the Creator, are referred to as *God* in this book. I extend an abundance of blessings, heartfelt love, and gratitude to everyone, as you respond in heart-resonating urgency.

"Dogmas of the past do not apply to the stormy present."
—ABRAHAM LINCOLN
PRESIDENT'S MESSAGE TO CONGRESS, 1862

"If you see your path laid out in front of you – Step one, Step two, Step three – you only know one thing...it is not your path. Your Path is created in the moment of action. If you can see it laid out in front of you, you can be sure it is someone else's path. That is Why you see it so clearly."

~ JOSEPH CAMPBELL ~

PART I

The Mundane Incubator

The Journey Begins . . .

"A journey of a thousand miles must begin with a single step."
—Lao Tsu

One's spiritual journey evolves out of one's life experiences—the background foundation, the subtleness of the mundane, *where the profound incubates.* What is it that drives one's love and joys and connects the pieces into a meaningful whole? Could it be the soulful threads of spirit, the essence in all that is, the awesomeness of connection, the wonders of nature and creation? Spiritual growth flows out of life's choices; choosing to know one-self is essential, and is done by obtaining an educated conscience through lifetime tools of leverage, discernment, and sound decision-making. You will find these simple but effective and everlasting tools and outlines here in this book.

Often, spiritual growth is seen as "doing holy or religious things." In reality, it is an inside job! I'll always remember the time I challenged the parish priests regarding a lack of programs for initiating spiritual growth in our parish. The year was 1990. The pastor's response was, "Oh, but we *do* have them—there are more people attending our morning and weekly rituals than before." When I stated that that was not spiritual growth, I was verbally attacked in anger and disbelief. An explanation was not an option and would have been a waste of my energy. A limited mind is a safe but closed mind. Being safe is about survival or having things the way they have always been. Risk is an element of growth. To be open-minded is to have good self-esteem and an openness to the new, to what is possible but not yet here. Uncertainty is the master of creativity; certainty is already here, already done; there is no risk. With no risk, there is no possibility. To live life is to cycle back and forth from certainty to uncertainty. (Once manifested, it then becomes certain, so we can cycle into uncertainty again in the continuity of ongoing growth.) Once we have mastered something, new possibilities become a spontaneous occurrence. One's free will chooses the safety of the old or opens to the possibility present in the new. Nothing is ever as good as it can be!

To cycle around and around in the old stagnates growth. To live life fully, and for continuity in ongoing growth, always choose the new, the path less traveled, even break ground and go where no one has ever been—to possibility! Today, the healing of humanity involves moving beyond dogmas, transcending the ego, and breaking the heart wide open to the sacred way of being and living—or fading away with the old world of destructive patterns and stagnation. The choice is here now. The timing is urgent; the cosmos is waiting.

Building an ongoing, loving resonance with others, to co-create in service to a better world, from the essence of the heart in a community of union is to experience sacred ground, pulsating the sacred synergy of heart-based love into the universe. This new way of being will wipe away the patterns of the past and initiate healthy new patterns, creating a better world for all—an *essential transition*.

I was moving into uncertainty at the time that I had angered the pastor. I had already made the decision that the time had come to move on, to seek environments of openness and spiritual awareness. This meant abandoning all efforts at initiating greater parish spirituality and a separation from a twenty-year structure that I had outgrown. When you no longer fit, it's time to move on. It's like leaving the tribal family. Because you want to move on, they often think there is something wrong *with you,* and they become defensive.

Stagnation is not beneficial; to grow in the spirit, one must step out of line from the familiar path and habitual traits on automatic replay.

Here in the Earth School, we are spiritual beings having human experiences. Our inner work *is* our spiritual work. To know oneself is the beginning step. Healing our wounds, moving past our programming and emotional baggage, and recovering our authentic self is a huge and necessary step, opening the mind and preparing our spirit for profound experiences in the awesomeness of divine source. Deprogramming and moving out of denial is a necessary process of inner growth.

A holistic life coach can help one to open psychological blocks, process and heal wounds, and transcend the ego. Self-help is abundant too. The alternative is to stagnate in the survival mode of development, clinging to old beliefs and toxic energies of the past because doing so feels comfortable and sustains a neediness to be right.

♥

"Knowing others is intelligence; knowing yourself is true wisdom. Mastering others is strength; mastering yourself is true power."
—Tao Te Ching

Reflections

What is germinating within *your* "mundane incubator"? Is a birth evolving? Is the spirit nudging you through a deep inner desire for something deeply meaningful to surface? Is the mundane of daily routine zapping your energy? Perhaps there is a busyness that prevents you from feeling *anything*.

Do you have a gnawing, empty feeling, like an empty hole needing to be filled, but so far, nothing works? Have you considered what is missing for you to birth and evolve in greater depth of consciousness? Perhaps there is numbness or an unconscious fear of change. Perhaps you very much wish to have new experiences but either don't know how to begin or fear what others will think. I have also met people who are simply not interested in knowing (total avoidance).

Whatever you are experiencing, know that you are a seed of humanity. To heal the self is to heal humanity. The energy vibration of one's being reaches far beyond the self; vibrations of *you* (your energy) go forth into the universe like a conduit of electro-waves.

What type of energy do you transmit to the universe every moment of every day? Is it loving and sacred or dense? The universe supports creative efforts to heal emotional pain, numbness, repetitive emotional stagnation; to grow, to change, to come alive in the spirit, to love self and all mankind. All it takes is deep desire, intentions, and seeking.

Everything is exposed in the world today; there is nowhere to hide the unethical or untruths. When we change our attitude, we change our life! "*When everything changes, change everything!*" (Book title: Neale Donald Walsh, author). Self-esteem is the by product of emotional healing, which is necessary to transcend the ego and move into the sacred essence of the heart. This is a **huge difference from the ego-powered energy of the false self.**

The essence of Source dwells within and incubates there until we evolve, give birth to the profound, and awaken the sacred simplicities lying beyond self-imposed limitations. We need to be aware of limitations that sustain lifelong, programmed boundaries.

I encourage everyone to discover their "mundane incubator," awaken to the emerging treasures within, and discover their authentic self. Give birth to a new way of being, a new emergent freedom of sacred energies, *a heart-based love for all things and everyone*. Breathe deeply! Relax . . . then take the leap!

Everyone has greatness, divinity, and holiness as a being of the Source. Humanity is healing through our journey in consciousness; going beyond controls of the ego—our ego and man's egoist and dominating dogmas—which constrict spiritual awareness and in turn, prevent advancement of the soul. As Scripture states, "The truth shall set you free" (*John 8:32 English Standard Version*), opening a constraining mindset and allowing a heart-based infinitude of unifying love; a spiraling, illuminating, evolving spiritual frequency forever resonating in divine abundance. All of this is a journey, not an arrival.

Come, celebrate the awesomeness of unifying resonance of small, sacred communities, where vibrating cosmic light converges on pioneering, love-pulsating hearts, co-creating humanity's sacred destiny. Time is urgent. It is simple to begin! ♥

♥ Further insight at *www.TheEssentialCode.com* ♥

PART II

Change, The Only Constant

"It is not the strongest of species that survive, nor the most intelligent, but the one most responsive to change."
—CHARLES DARWIN

Denial to Discernment

For centuries, the effects of alcohol were not understood; alcohol was even looked on and presented in society as sophisticated just a half-century ago. The average person did not understood alcoholism as a disease, or alcohol as an addictive substance, or a drug to be controlled. Society has since been educated on its effects. But even now, there needs to be easily available information regarding the fact that once one becomes sober (for example, via the twelve-step program of AA), there still remain the dysfunctional behavior patterns that pass from generation to generation. There is still work to be done—work that enables one to no longer need Alcoholics Anonymous as a crutch, to discover and develop the true self, and to enable profound growth of one's spirit and soul.

I was on a journey that awakened my own denial and the trials of recovery, along with the pains of healing. For me, it was a five-year process. But the journey also gave me insight into the mysterious behaviors and dysfunctional patterns of our existing human condition, the profound breadth and depth of the collective spirit.

Self-empowerment and awareness develop through education, experience, and personal will, by moving through the "internal journey." To truly know one-self is how profound spiritual awareness is realized. **It is *always* about the self!** It is only the self that can create a deeper relationship with the Source. Religious rituals enhance a sense of well-being, but do not and cannot awaken the authentic self.

There is a process in India that began in a small home and became so successful in creating The Oneness Blessing: The Power in the Evolution of Consciousness, it has since grown to be a university campus. Over 90 percent of this university's work is processing the history of participants, the healing of childhood hurts and repressed pain (Arjuna Ardagh, *Awakening into Oneness*. Sounds True Publications, 2007). Healing the human condition is a universal challenge and a necessity to successful evolutionary, co-creative manifestation.

When we are exposed to something we don't want to know about (our denial in play), defensive behavior surfaces to protect us from knowing. As long as one doesn't know, one doesn't have to do anything about it. Once one knows, then one can no longer ignore it; to change usually means experiencing pain, which no one wants to do. One can grow 'kicking' (battling stressors), or one can choose to *flow* in faith. **Emotional pain is a symptom of the need for inner growth**; blame, shame, and excuses are often one's defense. We have the free will to choose self-growth or remain in denial. Remaining in denial will stagnate one's development and further instills old paradigm habits.

One of the greatest challenges is being able to recognize and work through the concept that emotional pain is a call to inner growth. One cannot blame others or anything outside of oneself for one's inner pain. It is all about how you process it. Inner pain is one's catalyst to spiritual growth and transformation. **To**

heal, denial must be *owned.* **What is not owned cannot be transformed!**

There are many publications available to pursue self-knowledge. Just do an online search for "Adult Children of Alcoholics" and visit *www.johnbradshaw.com* to review some 2,500 selections in each about the various behaviors involved. I have heard that John Bradshaw's videos are mandatory viewing in many prisons. His works are excellent and are written in layman's language. Simply not having our needs met as a child can create the wounded inner child that we carry with us all our adult life. We require processing of our shadow side to heal, to discover our essence, our inner peace, and to further our spiritual evolution.

Forgiveness is what we do for the self: to forgive oneself, to forgive others does not mean we forget; it means we release the toxic energy within. To forgive is to let go of whatever shadow is harboring within, moving on to a healthy mind and happier state of being.

Significant to dysfunctional behaviors, which you may identify with, are addictions. ***Addiction: anything that prevents one from internal growth—can't let go to grow!*** These include drinking, abusive relationships, sex, even good activities like religion, exercise, sports, etc. (People become addicted to the short-term high.) Also, children are often exposed to an environment of "don't feel, don't think, don't talk." For example, in the face of a drunken parent, children might be told, "Nothing is wrong. Ignore what you see, hear, feel, and go about your business (of play, etc.)." Thus, denial sets in due to the denial of everyone's reality. Unmet needs in dealing with *'what is'* creates dysfunctional behaviors that pass on from generation to generation, until one discovers their denial and recovers the true self.

Internationally known sports figure Tiger Woods has exposed the world to what it means to come out of denial.

Since he is a public figure, the owning of his denial had to be a public event. Everyone who participated in this media frenzy defined not Tiger but their own level of ignorance of the human condition. Most people have dysfunctional patterns of some sort and are often—some obviously—in denial.

Tiger came out of denial through counseling and publicly owned his dysfunctional behavior of sexual addiction. He shared his plan to return to rehab for further healing. Coming out of denial is a very emotional and painful experience— one of letting go of role-playing and transitioning into one's authentic self. Discovery is not a rose garden; that is why so many individuals refuse to come out of denial. Recovery takes time, as does healing! Tiger wisely made no promises of when he would be playing golf again. He was just beginning the healing process. The process brings one into one's spirit self, shedding the false self and human conditioning—the role-playing or script that he or she has been living—the dysfunctional attitudes and behaviors of the false self.

Because Tiger Woods is a public figure, the world has the opportunity to observe this process. He needs great strength, which the rehab work enabled, along with time for his healing.

Tiger also needed great strength to face the other false selves who criticize and place blame and shame—who are devoid of understanding or the ability to support him in his decision to recover and heal. Once he achieves his goal, he will be a different person, and his intuitive, creative abilities will return.

The ego will be in transition, and the lack of perfectionism will be more tolerable. We are all striving to be the very best we can be, to develop our highest potential. When the ego is driving us, it's often painful to accept our limitations or even a bad day.

Tiger Woods will come back a better, and in time, a happier and more compassionate person than he has ever been. It is in experiencing pain that we learn compassion for the pain of others. Is anyone ready to own their personal recovery process? Addiction, again, is anything that prevents one from ongoing inner growth (the discovery of the spirit self, the authentic, whole self. Most addictive are the things that one can achieve a high from, such as exercise, running, religion, another person, sex, alcohol, drugs, extreme sports, any habit that allows one to be in avoidance of responsibility and ongoing personal development.)

Eventually, Tiger will arrive at a place where he will feel deep gratitude for his journey through pain, to the other side, with the realization that he could not be the person or spirit-self he was born to be, without his journey through pain. Pain is often the catalyst to crisis, and the chaos from the crisis is the evolutionary driver to growth and change.

In regards to the women involved in Tiger's affairs, they enabled his addiction and their own. Their language of blame and shame and defensiveness avoids self-responsibility. Game playing is always a counterproductive behavior. The women have the free will to choose the same process Tiger did.

Judgment, blame, and shame are egoic responses, whereas discernment, a response from an *educated conscience*, is based in psychological and spiritual truths, and bridges the connection in man's human condition, personal behaviors, and our spiritual being-ness. As you read on, you will discover the tools for obtaining an educated conscience, a priceless step toward the authentic self.

By Divine Design

Our journey is in our Creator's hands. The circumstances that I willingly accepted, that came to me without warning, were the very circumstances that created a leap in my spiritual journey, a growth process that took a decade to unfold. Upon reflection,

I have no doubt that our journey to the Source is enabled through absolutely everything that life brings to us. It is not a pleasure trip but one that creates gratitude from the worst of pain, as well as the greatest of joys. *This is an example that the divine binaries present in nature and the universe is mysteriously present in the mundane of life as well.* A profound and divine presence reveals the interconnectivity of all creation. The cosmology of spirituality; seeing with the third eye!

During a fourth grade parent meeting, in preparation for our son's sacrament of first penance, a very wise parish priest introduced me to Lawrence Kohlberg's stages of moral development. I was totally fascinated. The presentation created clarity in some of the church dogmas, initiated the freedom to shop for a confessor of wisdom and understanding, and created clarity regarding the sacrament of penance. To this day, I have not found another parish priest who understands the stages of moral development or has insight into its value as an asset to the church institution (the foundation of Vatican II changes) and society at large.

It has been my experience that priests involved in higher education and teaching ministries do have knowledge of Kohlberg's stages, but it remains a mystery whether they have insight into the influence that the stages had on the Vatican. Likely contributing to this condition was the small amount of psychology present in the curriculum for the seminarians in preparation for priesthood. (Hopefully, the mandatory curriculum has since changed. At that time, I was told it was about four hours of psychology, and the rest of the four-year prep was theology.)

In my mind, one parish priest made a huge difference. Knowing what I know now, it is not out of the realm of possibility that the other parish priests, including the pastor, did not possess this insight or understanding, making it difficult to initiate effective teaching consistency. The following year, the program leadership changed, and this valuable information was omitted.

In an Advanced Morality class, I was informed by a Catholic professor and tribunal lawyer of a document in the Vatican titled "Baptizing Kohlberg" (who was Jewish). He taught us that it was Kohlberg's stages of moral development that gave the pope and the Vatican the insight and courage to review outdated dogmas and church structure, and to call for a Vatican II. These were *decisions that resulted in a new religion in this historic universal church*.

Kohlberg took the same twenty questions around the world, obtaining data that collectively structured his stages of moral development. At the time of the survey, the United States had the highest reasoning level, at levels four and five (Law & Order and Social Contract). Other countries fell between levels one and four(Reward/Punishment, Reciprocity,& Approval levels). People in the United States were approximately 80 percent at level four and 12 to 15 percent at level five, with the other 5 or 6 percent at level six (Conscience & Principles. I believe the survey represents the development stages around 1950. Third world countries were on the lower levels of reasoning. Ongoing growth continues in a slow, developmental process. (We are, and have been, at war in countries with lower levels of reasoning.)

Kohlberg's stages are ways of looking at the process of justice; they are not concerned with helping people act morally, but with stimulating moral *thinking*. No one's thought is completely at a single level; most adults in our society were operating at levels four and five. The social context (the values, principles, and behavior patterns) in which people are reared is a strong learning influence. Furthermore, people can only understand reasoning at one level above their own and do not comprehend reasoning two levels above.

See Appendix A for typical comments at each stage, on select topics, for deeper insight.

Three Conscience-Forming Tools

Tool #1
Moral Development (Lawrence Kohlberg's stages of moral development)

STAGE I— Pre-Conventional (Selfishness—)	**Level 1. Reward—Punishment** Right and wrong determined by reward or punishment.	**ID—Child stage** Not much recognition of community or developed sense of what community is
(Judgment by consequences)	**Level 2. Reciprocity** Eye for an eye. You scratch my back, and I'll scratch yours.	(same as above)
STAGE II— Conventional Stage (Social order—socially permitted & accepted.) 3 (Judgment by intention)	**Level 3. Approval Stage** Good (nice) boy/girl. Guided by the approval of others: what pleases & helps others.	**Super-ego—Parent Stage** Recognition of community and significant people
(Judgment by existing law, support of law enforcement: authority orientation.)	**4. Law and Order** Right & wrong is determined by the law (rules). Break the law and you should be punished, or pay for it.	**Parent Stage** (same as above)
STAGE III Post-Conventional 5(Expressed in the U.S. Constitution.) Laws flow out of the contract.	**Level 5. Social Contract** The law, yes . . . but sometimes for the sake of a higher good the law must be transcended (go beyond).	**Adult ego** Just community- Human welfare— Principality

Level 6. Conscience-Principles   **A sense of self;**

6 (Abstract—   Universality—what is right &   informed and
No prescriptions for   just by universal principles.   educated
behavior but universal   The educated and informed   conscience
principles of justice   conscience determines moral   formation
and equality of human   decisions according to ethical
rights, respect for   principles.
dignity of human
beings as individuals.

♥_____♥

MORAL DEVELOPMENT (Lawrence Kohlberg's Stages of Reasoning)

Tool #1

MORAL REASONING with NOTED APPLICATIONS

Pre-Conventional
STAGE 1   <u>Level 1. Reward-Punishment</u>   <u>ID- Child Stage</u>

1.(Selfishness)   Right and wrong determined by   Not much
   Judgment by   reward and punishment   recognition of
   consequences   community-

        Average development age 1-2

        <u>Level II. Reciprocity</u>

2. (same as   Eye-for-an-eye. You scratch   Undeveloped
     above)   my back and I'll scratch   sense of what
       yours.   community is-

Some third world countries. Mafia; crime figures -

Conventional
STAGE II   <u>Level III Approval</u>   <u>Super ego — Parent Stage</u>

3.(Social order -   Good (nice) boy/girl   Recognition of community
Socially permitted   Guided by approval of   and of <u>significant</u> people.
and accepted.)   others; what pleases
(3.Judgment by   and helps others.
intentions.   Ages 9-12 and some adults

        <u>Level IV Law and Order</u>   <u>The Parent Stage</u>

4 (Judgment by   Right & wrong is determined by   *Significant other*
existing law,   law (rules). Break the law and   = people of
support of law   you should be punished, or pay   Authority
       for it.

      Authority - Church as Parent - *Obedience by the Rule*
   1950: 80% of US Populace   **PRE-VATICAN CHURCH -**
          THE Baltimore Catechism

STAGE III Post-Conventional

5 (Expressed in	5. Social Contract	Adult Ego Stage
The Constitution.	The law yes, but sometimes	Just community –
Laws flow out	For the sake of a higher good	Human Welfare –
Of the contract.	The law must be transcended	Principality
	(to go beyond)	
1950: 12-15% of U.S.	**Higher Good = Life, a Healthy Existence**	

V A T I C A N II aligned Church Law with Level 6 - but stopped all change just prior to changes in outdated Hierarchal Law –

	6. Conscience – Principles	A sense of self -
6 (Abstract –	Universality – what is right	Informed and
Not prescriptions	and just by universal	educated
for behavior but	principles. The educated	conscience
universal principles	and informed conscience	formation.
of justice and	determines moral decisions	
equality of human	according to ethical principles.	
rights, respect for		
dignity of human		
human beings as individuals.		

**One's educated conscience guides decision making; concerned
with Ecology, World Peace, Essence Guided Actions,
and The *Essential Code***

Note: Church Institution must always stand for the highest of values and principles.

The individual is called to decisions through an educated and informed conscience. **Adults are called to make adult decisions regarding their faith response. Circumstances may, at times create decisions that transcend (church) law, or rules. (No sin is committed). What is OK for one, is NOT OK for another.**

♥ *It is the 'why', not the 'what' that determines a just action.*
♥

The stages and levels *do not apply to chronological age*, but to how one reasons. A ten-year-old and a fifty-year-old may reason at the same level. Ages listed on the form indicate the average age of developing youth. We love nine-to-twelve-year-old youths—they wish to please others (meet approval). When teens come to the "law and order" stage, striving to find their own self-identity, the challenges of growth often bring conflict. Break the law and you will be legally held responsible, but you may not have done anything *morally* wrong. *Life, and the healthy development of life, is of the highest priority* in discerning decisions that transcend the law (or rules).

Apply Kohlberg's stages to the Catholic Church's institutional structure, and it becomes obvious why there was mass confusion when Vatican II was released and why some are still confused about their religion. The Vatican II changes placed its values at the highest standard, level six, but the people (who *are* the Church) are at various levels in the reasoning process. Many do not, and cannot, operate at the Church's level six reasoning (and some cannot understand it), which justly and forever changed the Catholic religion.

The hierarchy is in the same developmental dilemma. The greatest problem is not what people could understand, but the fact that the goals of Vatican II were cut short when Pope John XXIII passed away, prior to the completion of Vatican II. The new pope, Paul VI, refused to allow further changes in the dogmas—which regarded the hierarchal structure, including the fallibility question and power of the pope.

The unfinished changes denied the Church an all-inclusive approach. It also prevented the Church from fulfilling the agreement of the council, which was to complete what Vatican II had started and intended: to bring the Church to a balanced universal structure that went beyond the outdated dogmas and power structures of the medieval ages.

Science and spirituality agree that universal principles apply to everything. Brian Swimme, at the California Institute of Integral Studies, teaches that at the very beginning, the "Big Bang" had everything needed to create a perfectly balanced universe. Everything needed was present in that moment. And that the universe is so delicately balanced that even the *tiniest of change in any one chemical* would mean that our world would not exist. This demand for balance flows throughout all creation and applies to all things, including the mundane life of mankind. An unbalanced structure cannot thrive but slowly decays and fades away. (The spirit never stagnates!) Reality continually proves this principle: mismanaged corporations, unbalanced structures in organized religion, marriage structures, diseases of the human body, everything is subject to the principles and delicate balance present in all creation. The human body is a mini universe, with the same principles.

The Church's institution still has an unbalanced structure. There are still power struggles to keep things "as they have always been," using irrational, obsolete, and outdated reasoning, creating a false sense of credibility. Vatican II enabled the people of the church to attain a higher level of values, while the hierarchy and powers of the pope remained structured according to the standards of the Baltimore Catechism and the medieval ages. *The Catholic Church, A Short History,* by Hans Kung, is a book that "tells the truth about the Catholic past for the sake of the church's future," according to reviewer James Carroll. The crises in the Catholic Church are well outlined in this short and informative publication.

~ *A Short Measure* ~

The following offers detailed insight on the Vatican II dilemma and the world's largest universal church as it stands today. In January 1959, Pope John XXIII announced his intentions, just three months after his election. Preparations began, and by June 1960, ten councils, or commissions, were established to study and coordinate the assigned requests from the pope. A central committee helped the pope to decide on subjects for debate in the council, as well as on the suggested rules of procedure. Two thousand five hundred priests were present at the council, the largest ever in the history of the Church. The fathers began their work with the guidance of the pope. Changes in the liturgy and language, the altar, sacraments, RCIA, liturgical year, music, art, social activities increase, Eastern church outreach, ecumenism, the unity of all Christians, and the Church in the modern world were all processed before Pope John XXIII passed on. His leadership was a wide-reaching, collaborative effort, using a circular style of leadership consisting of ten committees (versus the outdated pyramid style leadership of cascading dominance).

However, his successor, Pope Paul VI, voided all further changes with a dominating decision, going against the efforts and desires of the collaborative leaders. This left untouched the decisions for change in regards to the hierarchy, papal power, and the fallibility issue. (*The fallibility issue was the only subject of the 1870 Vatican I, which ended as soon as a favorable ruling regarding fallibility was pushed through.* For additional help and information in the application of Kohlberg's Moral Development, beyond the Catholic Church, see Appendix A.)

Vatican II was closed in October 1965. It was a short measure to the greatness that Vatican II had set out to attain. Today, the church still exists with an unbalanced and outdated leadership structure, largely unprepared to lead and educate the laity on the true meaning of the new cosmic energies and the newly formed religion.

It has been more than forty-five years, and much remains untouched and ignored. Leadership has become complacent, and parish structures are diminishing—as unbalanced structures tend to do. Absolute power stagnates absolutely. The reported growth of the church comes from evangelization efforts in third world countries, as the established areas of the church become spiritually stagnant with attendance slowly fading away.

I believe the Catholic Church is still the largest universal church in the world. It either influences or dismays a large portion of the world populace. The energy of the new world age requires a balanced, co-creating leadership structure at the top, a vital intervention for the spiritual evolution of the institution. Like many other unbalanced power structures, still in the old paradigm, the Church institution is buried in its obsolete power structure and likely will not evolve in harmony with divine cosmic energies of the twenty-first century.

♥ ~ ♥ ~ ♥

Tool#2
Historical Perspective of Decision-Making

Another source of useful interest is the *Historical Perspective of Decision Making,* an outline detailing a structure that separates unchanging values from the cases we deal with on a daily basis. To clarify and sustain a high standard of values guides one in making just, mature, and ethical decisions by separating the trivial and unimportant from what is significant. Many arguments cycle around and around the meaningless trivia with no vision of the underlying value that is to be sustained and clarified.

(Note that an adult response concentrates on high values and principles, while a pedagogy (adolescence) response concentrates on particulars—the rules/cases: see "Identity Outline," just ahead.)

Values	Need defining—should be first class (highest standard)
Principles	Need clarification—expresses principles
— — — — — — — — — — — — — —
Rules	Continual Reform—capsulate principles
Cases	Tests the rules—bring about variances to the rules

What is fundamentally important is the value, and to protect the value, we establish principles. Principles are then best expressed in human behavior by the established rules, which are then tested in real-life scenarios. As you go down the structure, each stage becomes more particularized and less universal, and therefore, less generally accepted. For example, nobody will really question the value of life, and few people will question the principle that life is to be respected. However, when this universal value is applied to specific scenarios, more people will find fundamentally reasonable grounds on which to disagree. They might say, for example, that the rule, "Don't perform abortion because it is taking a human life," doesn't apply to those cases of raped youth. In other words, the more specific these cases become, the less you will find a universal agreement. Therefore, one cannot apply a universal value to a specific case. For example, subjectively, you cannot call a person a murderer because you do not know the individual case (all of the elements that led to that person's moral decision). So you may subjectively judge what that person did as an objective wrong. However, God's decision on the matter is the objective truth—elements that transcend human discernment. What we can do is to constantly try to retain the values, which means defining and redefining and re-organizing our rules to make sure our principles adhere. (Ref: Advance Morality Course, Dennis Burns)

Tool#3
Self-Identity

The following is a "Self-Identity" outline with the dualities of childlike and adult traits.

SELF-IDENTITY (i.e., one's work environment/functional abilities)

AMORPHOUS (no concreteness: no form)	INTEGRATED
(Results of pedagogy) CHILD	(Results of androgogy) ADULT

Dependence
You owe me, show me, follower

Passivity
Who cares? So what? Not me!

Subjectivity
Bondage—at the mercy of

Ignorance
Blind, unaware, no idea

Small abilities
Limited opportunities, esteem
and energy

Few responsibilities
'not my job'

Narrow interests
Having it the way it has always been

Low risk factor—shallowness
Selfishness
What's in it for me

Self-rejection (exception)
I don't count, I'm not worthy or
good enough

Focus on PARTICULARS
Insignificance, blame, narrow
vision

Superfluous
Grandiose, Neediness, surface
vision

Imitation
Sham, pretense, unreal

Need for certainty
Stay in one's safety zone
'Don't rock the boat!'
Keep the status quo

Pedagogy process (child)

Autonomy
Self-starter—beyond need
for approval (squashed by
pedagogy methodology).

Activity
'get to' rather than 'have
to. Many irons in the fire

Objectivity
Emotional stability, aim,
ambition

Enlightenment
Informed, openness, teacher

Large abilities
Responsible, capable,
and energy energized

Many responsibilities
'Can do!' Variety is
'spice'.

Broad interests
Open to new—try anything
once.

High risk factor—balanced
Altruism
Will it help others?
Generosity

Self-acceptance
I'm great!..but not perfect
I am!

Focus on PRINCIPLES
Values, universal good,
visionary

Deep concerns
Simple, profound, bird's-eye
view.

Originality—Unconformity
Creative, unique,

Tolerance of ambiguity
Risk taker, detachment
trust, intuition, creative
visualization

Androgogy process (adult)

22

ANDROGOGY PROCESS = *The interest is on the individual*

Personal(individual) goals versus institutional goals:

Focus on the person . . . . and institution goals will take care of themselves. Success means interest is not the rehabilitation of the institution, but with the development, integrity, and potential of the people.

Per divine order—"People before things." Life and the preservation of life are of the highest value; things are never more important than the development, respect, and potential of the person. Human DNA reveals the message, "God Eternal Within" (Gregg Braden, *The God Code,* 2007). What's more important than the sacredness of life?

Balance equals trainable people with ability to risk, to change and creatively thrive on challenge versus workaholics with tunneled expertise. The amount of one's education often has little to do with such traits as innovation and self-initiative.

Institutions and corporations often breed pedagogy-type environments (i.e., cone-shaped, pyramid leadership style). A cutting-edge institution/corporation quickly moves into andragogy environments with ongoing, evolving development and team-building leadership methodologies. The changes necessary for a sustainable future demand this type of focus, where a caring, loving, and compassionate environment nourishes and develops others in reaching their potential, while honoring the sacredness of their being. In turn, individuals are responsible for incarnating the sacred way of being. This requires transitioning from the pedagogy response into the andragogy state of being—**a transition that can happen through entrainment (practice in the entirety; a sequential continuity) of the tools and insight offered.**

These three valuable outlines can be helpful tools in decision-making. They can assist in the recognition of systemic thought formation and the differentiation between particulars and principles. This differentiation sustains a high standard of values (the principle) while allowing variables of the particulars to be discussed and discerned as to their importance and application in sustaining the principle. The question to ask in any dialogue is, "What are we talking about—the principle (of the highest of standards), or the particulars that either sustain or destroy what we hold valid and dear (our values)?"

As stated, principles rarely change, while particulars (which we give most of our attention to) change according to the cases, and cases bring about changes in the rules (that uphold and sustain a high standard of values). Alert: Sometimes, too much focus on particulars could destroy the value(s). Listen carefully to political issues and debates around the world!

I like using the three outlines (three Conscience-Forming Tools). They are simple and easier to use than pages and pages of text and contain adequate "gems and nuggets" for learning. They can be easily reviewed in a few short minutes to quickly refresh one's memory. They are unaffected by time, *will always be applicable to the human condition*, and will always assist in acquiring an informed conscience.

I found that in my transitions and discoveries along my spiritual path (is there any other?), tools to guide overall decision-making are a treasure. I believe that sound ethical tools give us more leverage for discernment and ethical justice in all issues of life.

> *"Change is the essence of life. Be willing to surrender*
> *what you are for what you could become!"*
> —UNKNOWN AUTHOR

Demo: Tools, US Constitution, and Health Care

Following is an exercise using the Historical Decision-Making Structure, the US Constitution, and the US health care bill. First, a reminder of our Founding Fathers' document, the document that made the United States a country that people from all over the world want to be a part of—the US Constitution—which upholds our high values: the right to life, liberty, and the pursuit of happiness (our *wellbeing* is a synchronism of happiness).

These values came out of something called natural law. Under natural law, all human laws are to be judged on the basis of how closely they conform to the laws of the Supreme Being and nature. Natural law holds truth to be self-evident, that all men are created equal, that they are endowed by their Creator with certain inalienable rights, which among these are life, liberty, and the pursuit of happiness.

We are spiritual people by nature. The US Constitution was founded on spiritual values, not religious, but on nature itself. In today's terminology, nature is declared a natural process of cellular creation. A cell is life. Cells are a free entity, valued for their differentiation and evolutionary potential. We are a cell in our cosmic and earthly environment, cells that encompass and equate all humanity. Every human being has inherited the natural right to the spontaneous evolution of life, liberty, and the pursuit of happiness. From the very beginning, the US government was sent forth in service to the people, by the people, *with* the people. Congress and the president are mandated to uphold the values and principles of the US Constitution. If government fails to uphold and protect these values, the populace could justifiably overthrow the government through impeachment of leadership.

Liberty means freedom. Freedom is not freedom to do what you want; freedom is earned. Everyone is subject to responsibility and accountability. It is the responsibility of all citizens to actively assure that their government upholds the US constitutional values; to be informed and knowledgeable of the background and values of their electoral candidates, and to vote wisely for leaders who will responsibly represent the people.

US Constitution and Universal Health Care Applied to the Historical Decision-Making Structure

Value: LIFE (US Constitution)—of the highest priority
Principle: LIBERTY (US Constitution)—Upholds our highest values
The pursuit of Happiness (US Constitution)—Upholds our rights
- Freedom of choice in sustaining life
- The right to pursue personal well-being (happiness).

Rules/Laws: (The "particulars"—over-focus here can destroy the Values and principles—what we hold dear in life).
- Renewal (to know again, but in a new way):
Health reform (assure Constitutional justice)
- US Universal Health System that upholds US Constitution:
     Universal **Health Care = Program for All:**
     - Freedom of choice—Private Insurance or Government Program
     - Insurance premiums and out-of-pocket medical expenses as a tax credit for all = *Universal* Plan

Cases: Bring about changes to the rules.
- Lack of waste management: Clinics and doctors overcharging the system.

- Unconstitutional Medicare management by a presidential Board (rumored possibility) is subject to partisan rule and Presidential control. Constitutional US leadership mandates rule by the people, with the people—that is why we have a Congress elected by the people, to speak for them. Presidential control of health is unethical.

Because of who we are, a nation governed by our Constitution, we do not have the liberty to compare or adapt our health care to that of other countries. With the financial state of our country in 2012, a true universal health plan is not even a possibility. Given knowledgeable leadership, councils of financial genius and US constitutional abilities to co-create peace in the world, a true universal health care can manifest over time. What Congress decides is good for us citizens is also applicable to Congress! Congress should not have a separate, elite plan just for them. The US handouts are out of proportion and out of balance. Everything has to change.

England has a government-run health care system that provides excellent clinical and preventive care, with free pharmaceuticals. There are issues with their 'Blanket Policy' and limitations on surgeries, specialized situations, and timing for services.

Sustaining the best quality of life possible for all is the goal and the constitutional right of every US citizen: to have a balanced, just, and caring system, free of rationing of needed services, professional gouging, unethical judgments, and a demand for integrated medical practices with retraining of doctors and caretakers. We definitely need a reframing of the drug companies and the current drug system, for any type of health care system to thrive. We are being controlled by a structure of greed. The American people need to take back their natural rights for natural wellbeing and happiness, based on the fundamental meaning of our Constitution.

♥ ～ ♥ ～ ♥

Freedom Definded—2011

Responsible freedom creates our quality of life. Freedom does not simply give anyone the right to do what they want. Freedom is earned by responsible decision-making and behavior. Below, the previous Tools are applied to responsible, earned freedom, the US Constitution, and values of the highest order:

Value = FREEDOM TO CHOOSE (Value of highest quality) *A sacred privilege!*

    Infinite Possibilities—Co-Creativity—Conscious Evolution

Principles = *FREEDOM DEMANDS RESPONSIBILITY (Clarifies, expresses values)*

-   *Responsible, accountable action for self, earth, humanity:*
  All is one; diversity in unity with enduring capacity to
  co-create a sustainable earth, peace-filled communities,
  a loving wisdom, and incarnate the sacred oneness of all.

Rules = *FREEDOM IS UPHELD AND GUIDED BY THE RULES (capsulate principles)*

    Rules sustain our principles; when populace can implement
    values and principles on their own, then rules will not
    be necessary (i.e., heart-to-heart communities of communion).

Cases = *FREEDOM IS TESTED AGAINST THE RULES BY OUR ACTIONS (brings about variances to the rules in order to uphold our values)*

- *Behavior and experiences—are they aligned with the sacred privilege and principles of freedom, the US Constitution and the loving energies emerging in the new world age?*

FREEDOM'S HISTORIC PERSPECTIVE

FREEDOM DEMANDS . . .
Responsible, accountable action, the highest of values,
privileges earned, and a life lived beyond fear.

FREEDOM STANDS . . .
When human diversity unites in harmony and peace,
celebrating life, individual achievements, and the right to
choose.

FREEDOM ENDURES . . .
Each time it is upheld (often in blood and heroic sacrifice)
in honor of its treasure and the laws that guide and protect it.

FREEDOM REIGNS . . .
Each time the oppressed are liberated, enabling responsible
decision-making, freedom to be, and respect for self and all.

FREEDOM IS . . .
An eternal and inalienable right, a spirit embedded in the
soul . . . a divine gift—inspiring one's unique, creative flow.
We honor those whose ultimate sacrifice, grace, and suffering
sustains this gift; our hearts swell with deep and sincere
GRATITUDE for the freedom to live and love . . . and *be!*

—ARVETTA SOUZA 2004

PART III

An Educated Conscience Is Priceless

"In matters of conscience, the law of the majority has no place"
—Mohandas Gandhi

An educated conscience formed from a high standard of values and sound moral reasoning easily can determine and clarify just action. When we consider *what* someone has done, we tend to focus on the particulars, often followed with judgments and blame orientation. When we move to understand *why* a person has chosen a particular course of action, we can then use value-oriented discernment from life-sustaining principles (such as understanding and compassion, love and forgiveness). The *why* reveals circumstances, develops insight, and enables just decisions.

In legal matters, where a law has been broken, one will likely pay the penalty of the law, (Level Four, Kohlberg), but the *why* may bring one to transcend the law for a higher good, for a higher moral and just decision (Level Five). A higher good is defined by the highest value, which is life itself, and that which would enable a stable and healthy existence. All decisions either add to life or destroy life, adding either light or darkness to the journey.

Understanding the stages of human development helps one to understand actions hold growth potential. Stagnation of one's developmental progress creates dis-ease and unmet needs. An unhealthy existence in a decaying environment demands new conditions for meeting needs and higher values for healthy living. The spirit never stands still; at our core is an inner knowing of personal needs, an inner voice guiding one in sacred, just, and life-affirming decisions—pulling one in a direction that one may not be readily willing to follow. It is easier to stay in the familiar and safe box of what has always been, rather than risk the unknown change that allows new ventures in self-development. Knowledge about life is contagious. Once on the journey, one becomes inspired to know more and experience more. Be aware! Pain is always involved in a fully lived life; avoidance of pain results in stagnation. Time never stands still; it waits for no one. Try to realize that pain is often a blessing that says, "Yes, I am alive!" Pain is a catalyst to profound growth.

An educated and informed conscience is a priceless asset, and for some, a lifetime of learning. Prayerful reflection on one's experiences, education in moral decision-making, a high standard of values, and understanding aspects of human development and behavior are all attributes to an educated conscience. One doesn't have to spend long hours in formal classes to gain a basic, foundational knowledge of this spiritual path. Studying, reviewing, and applying the basics, over and over again, with a deep desire for learning and gaining greater spiritual insight are all part of the developmental process. Everyday experiences offer opportunities for learning and applying the basics on a day-to-day basis. Prayer and daily spiritual practice is a given.

This does not mean religion, but meditations that resonate in the inner sanctuary and readings that evolve soulful insight. Spiritual consciousness develops over time. Time and energy spent on educating the conscience is precious. The stepping stone to profound spiritual depth requires successful growth in values and decision-making and formation of an educated conscience.

The outlines and charts presented in this book are lifetime tools to be further investigated and studied. The Catholic Church has always upheld the primacy of conscience, but even today it is a well-kept secret in most parishes, just as the influence of Kohlberg's stages of moral development was also a secret, unknown or ignored by those responsible for educating the laity. Of course, to educate the laity would then expose the structural imbalance.

Insights and Transitions

It is sometimes said that too much education is dangerous. I believe that knowledge is good and that too much knowledge without conscious intelligence is dangerous. *Intelligence* is evolution turned inward toward the human mind. We are no longer in the age of the first Internet and sharing of data around the world; humanity has evolved into the "Age of Conscious Intelligence." (*Referring to the Historical Graph: Global Trends from* Canticle of the Cosmos *video program by Brian Swimme; the graph is coming up in a few pages.*)

What does this information have to do with spiritual development? Most people today know that the brain has two parts for processing information: the left brain and the right brain. The left brain processes logic and information. The right brain processes the intuitive, spiritual, and creative aspects— with the two working together to manifest reality. The "Age of Conscious Intelligence" (the "now") is an age of unlimited potential, an inward journey of co-creative energy; a right-brain activity. This indicates that we are moving into an era of great spiritual synergy, a holistic approach where the co-creative synergy of the whole is greater than the sum of its parts.

Our intuition connects us to God, or Source, as does the influencing cosmic energy of Aquarius: a spiritual energy now in force (following the two thousand-year influence of Pisces and Aries, energies of war and deeper human development). In this new world age, humans will be more inclined to evolve in their spiritual path and to experience a more holistic and connected sense of awareness. Humans will *see without seeing*— gaining in intuitive awareness of how everything is connected to everything else. Our developed intellect and informed conscience will begin to understand the illusions of the material and physical world, to know that everything is made of energy. Even the chair you sit on is made of energy, as well as the body "hosting" our being. *Our thoughts and heart-based feelings of love and compassion are powerful energy conduits.* Collectively, we have the power to create a sacred destiny and the peaceful world we have previously only dreamed of.

"Could it be that by shifting the way we feel, we not only affect, we determine our tuning to the resonant circuit of creation? This circuit is responsible for the quality of the signal that feeds each cell within our body. This circuit determines the vitality and well-being of each cell and the organs that the cells create. Is it possible that a feeling may determine the quality of that signal?" *(Gregg Braden, Walking Between the Worlds (1997, out of print, 67)*

Again, the principles of the universe apply to all things, including earth, humans, and our daily lives. We are 70 percent water and 30 percent solid matter, (all of which is *energy*). The earth, too, is 70 percent water and 30 percent solid matter. We are interconnected with all of creation. The Source energy is woven throughout the energy of all creation. So why limit one's faith to our mundane daily experience, drawing a straight line from man to God? Like the Church's institution, we, as spiritual beings, need *to shift our focus from an inner devotion to an active, outward inclusion of all that is.* The spiritual journey is an inward path, but with the awareness that our attitudes, celebrations, and faith are to be all-inclusive, to actively extend glory and gratitude for all that is. Not in just a few words, but as a holistic, evolutionary, new approach. Well-planned celebrations of this nature create an awesome resonance and "felt" life experiences of oneness! Echoes of the *Essential Code!*

Vatican II called adults to adult responsibility and to adult decisions regarding their faith. This required a "letting go" and deprogramming of a lifetime of beliefs and dependency on the church as parent, moving from a duty orientation to a freedom of choice and heartfelt desires.

While I was in the service of the Catholic Church, a meeting was arranged between the pastor and me to discuss, again, the need for spiritual development opportunities, which was one of our parish goals. Not being open to required changes of our new pastoral plan, the pastor said to me, without any compassion, "You are not one of us!" I couldn't believe what I had heard, coming from a leader in the church. In an instant forgiveness of his defensiveness, I dismissed what he had said. Then, a couple of years later, I came to realize that his statement was true, but not from the perspective in which it was given. I was definitely not a part of the status quo, nor did I possess a blanketed and closed mind, nor did I function at the status quo Level Three Faith Development, in which trust is confined within one's small group. At this level of faith, if you are an outsider and do not feed into the group, you are considered deviant; if you do feed into the group and the others don't agree with you, then you are still considered deviant. It's a no-win situation when your developmental level has evolved from that of the others in the group. You may recognize this scenario in your workplace, social groups, and family.

The great challenge of Vatican II resulted in the removal of laity absolutes, initiating individual, adult decision-making (cultures of obedience demand absolutes). The higher good in moral reasoning places life as the highest value and merges psychology and spirituality. (Kohlberg's stages represent a psychology of reasoning, merged in the high values of spirituality.) We must strive to look beyond rigid moral absolutes. This transcendence in decision-making creates circumspection—the ability to evaluate more accurately, to "look all around" and survey the whole situation. Absolutes and extreme beliefs contaminate the ability to consider extenuating and applicable factors, causing one to disconnect from reality.

Even the last seven commandments pertaining to man (the first three pertain to God) stated as absolutes—considering only the "what"—becomes an inadequate means for moral decision-making. With the last two levels of moral reasoning, along with an understanding of psychological and human development aspects, a balanced and just decision can be discerned and understood. In Neil Donald Walsh's channeled message, "A loving God does not make commands, but asks for commitments" (*Conversations with God,* 1996, 96–97). This is a huge difference and includes the same reasoning process.

Nothing in the world of an educated conscience is black and white or ruled from a blanket order for all. The human condition has evolved beyond medieval times, and science has proven that nothing pertaining to the human spirit can grow when stagnated in absolutism.

Scripture was conceived and written in an age long before the spiritual evolution of the masses. Current understanding of Scripture upholds the sacredness of accounts, and it is now aware that God is not a Santa Claus who gives gifts to the "good," but instead, an energy that works through people. Many Bible stories are parables that are related to spiritual truths, but the actual events did not occur. An updated understanding of the Bible is more than Bible study in the local church. Insight and revelations into the Bible can come from the many venues of research, study, historical and spiritual truths, and new knowledge that have now been revealed to mankind through the Essenes, Dead Sea Scrolls, books that were withheld from the Bible, and quantum physicists' research.

Those who do not wish to accept what is shared here are invited to follow that which they do understand. No one has to accept anything in this book that they are not ready or willing to accept. The writings here are for those who understand and seek the path to a deeper consciousness. Witnessing an intense and deeply profound journey of another can help to more readily identify our own journey. I share what I have experienced in my ongoing journey to know God, Source, universe, more clearly, and more dearly.

Throughout twenty-five years of ministry, service, education and learning, I possessed a great amount of love for the people. I understood how the spiritual limitations of parish leadership created an equal amount of limitations in spiritual growth among thousands of people who "didn't know what it was they didn't know"! Efforts to create greater insight through joint goal-setting efforts and program implementation became a real threat to the status quo—a status quo that was patronized by pastoral administration, solidifying a stagnating environment. The goals had been accepted and confirmed by the cardinal, with the regional bishop stating that these were the best parish plans they had ever read. However, this meant little to nothing to the administrative leadership. It was as if, in their pattern of denial, they didn't even know of the work the parishioners had accomplished.

After hitting walls over a three-year period, I turned my energy to preparing and facilitating day retreats. They were fun and were well attended. In this venue, I found the freedom to expand and create meaningful experiences and thought-provoking insights, receiving several compliments from attending professionals and laity alike. Affirmations were very much appreciated! The experiences were an affirmation of the spiritual hunger present within the laity.

Circular Leadership Style

A circle has no end; it is an eternal ring. "Circular means" is *making ongoing connections*—sharing responsibility (versus a 'means to an end'). The earth is an eternal circle, and the earth is a nurturing and compassionate entity—warm and life-giving. The same is true of the human circle; it is *relational*, it has a sphere of influence, it creates equality and promotes eye contact. ***Equality has to exist for intimacy to happen.*** One cannot form intimacy if one has a judgmental attitude. Rap groups (camaraderie gatherings), family dining, and support groups all gather to share in the nurturing and intimacy-building warmth of the circle.

The enclosed circle is suggestive of a return to the womb: a warmth and acceptance, an atmosphere for birthing new creations. "Circular means" places the emphasis on people and nature versus *things*. Understanding interdependency is important: each is responsible for self, and a nurturing and compassionate environment for self and others that is mutually dependent on one another and involved in one another.

Consensus is a *circular* process, a "both/and" strategy versus a means to an end (which is an "either/or" strategy). **Circular leadership** is a circle of people with a shared task, where the talents of everyone are invited and respected. Leadership will pass from one to another, according to their talents and abilities. Everyone knows who the *leader is,* and all work together to obtain a consensus of agreement. Circular resolutions and discernments take longer than a "Robert's Rule of Order," but results are of a higher value and create a desire to cooperate. (Holistic group dynamics is applied in all settings: corporate, sports, spiritual, and others.)

The following is the process of a circular-style leadership:

Consensus deductive reasoning process:
    Thesis—The Perfect State
            Antithesis—The Opposition
    Synthesis—The Compromise . . . {Thesis
            {Antithesis
            {Synthesis . . . Sometimes

over and over again–

The THESIS is the perfect state. The ANTITHESIS is the resistance. SYNTHESIS is deductive reasoning. To reach a synthesis is to go through a complete process, sometimes over and over again, until a consensual solution has been reached. This allows everyone to come together in unity to support the outcome. **In the deductive process of an evolutionary consensus group, the end result is aimed toward "Meta-Synthesis"—from an emerging form of systemics (holistic systems).**

Consensus does not mean 100 percent agreement, but issues are discussed, compromised, and worked through until agreement is obtained, and efforts made to compromise, where a very small number who cannot totally agree *can live with the decision, and support it!*

Members who have gained an educated conscience and can move into their essential self, versus the egoic or "local self," will easily transition in the compromising, consensus method of discernment. If a situation arises where one or two simply cannot accept the process, then an obvious split with the group has occurred. They are either out of sync with the co-creative purpose or do not fit within the group. If they absolutely cannot support the group, the alternative is to leave the group.

PYRAMID LEADERSHIP STYLE—A MEANS TO

AN END (A cone-shaped style)

The pyramid leadership style means that the leader is at the top, makes all decisions and they filter down, and dominates his subordinates. The decision-making process in this type of leadership is *Robert's Rules of Order.* This parliamentary form of decision-making works well in minor decisions and keeps order in large assemblies. However, it is not the best system for major decisions and team spirit. Often, it divides the people into winners and losers and often means that the losers are not given the opportunity to come to terms with and support the decision of the "other side." At best, the "losers" feel that it isn't really their decision. There is no compromising, and at worst, they feel angry and frustrated and begin to rip the decision as soon as they leave. In either case, they won't jump with ecstatic enthusiasm when the time comes to commit their time and energy into implementing the decision.

Leaders who have no concern for the feelings of their people are likely to be unaware of the feelings and disharmony within the organization. Unconscious leadership is indicative of a pedagogic pattern of the old world paradigm.

The advantages of the pyramid decision-making process are: works in large assemblies, good for finalizing decisions and reaching closures (final stage of deliberation). However, it has many disadvantages: most people don't understand the rules (in formal, large groups); can be overly formal; inhibits the flexibility required in group problem-solving; can be highly manipulative; can encourage process arguments (or "motion sickness"); is solution-oriented (versus agreement-oriented) and can polarize a group.

SUCCESS is:

- The progressive realization of a worthy ideal.
    - The preservation and enhancing of relationships while accomplishing results.
    - Doing what you predetermined to do and making it work!
    - Cooperation, cooperation, cooperation.

What doesn't fall within the above outline for success is: status quos, absolutes, dominating power, a pyramid style of leadership (often present in office settings, institutions, and organizational structures, and within some families), and significantly, the unfinished Vatican II plans voided by absolute power.

When you change your belief system, you change your life ("open the windows and let in fresh air"). Cooperation under absolute power is a simple obedience to rules (dogma). This is in contrast to cooperative team efforts. A prime example of circular leadership and joint decision-making is that of Pope John XXIII, when he organized ten decision-making bodies and included twenty-five hundred Fathers in the preparation and processing of Vatican II. Pope John XXIII was truly a blessed and powerful world leader, so much so that I think he should be elevated to a saint. His vision and leadership did more for the Catholic Church and the world than any other pope in history. He was, and still is, loved by the world.

Another tool in understanding human development and growth patterns is Eric Erickson's levels of psychosocial development. Erickson's stages merge with Kohlberg's stages of moral development to form the six levels of faith development (James Fowler's Six Levels of Faith Development).

Our journey toward maturity and spiritual development doesn't have to be one of unknowing. When we gain insight into the self and begin to understand where we are, where we are going, and what will take us there, our self-esteem and the grace to move onward strengthen the way to our intended path. When we depart from our childhood and adolescent inherited beliefs, we begin a radical shift from dependence to an educated conscience based on universal principles.

Eric Erickson's PSYCHOSOCIAL

DEVELOPMENT

At birth, we tend to tilt either toward the positive or the negative. For example, within the first nine months, the child would tilt toward basic trust if his needs have been met; if not, then he would tilt toward mistrust, the negative side. One will continue developing in this tilt until the Identity Stage (development of the personality through social interaction). At this point, if one is in the negative, (a sense of guilt, self-doubt, and lack of initiative) then he would have to go back to experience and develop each stage in the positive before he can go on to develop positively (a sense of pride, to feel capable and able to lead). Positive development goes from Basic Trust to Autonomy, Initiative, Industry, and Identity (as stated on the chart).

Eric Erickson Graph Psycho-Social Development

	PSYCHOSOCIAL CRISIS	RATIOS OF SIGNIFICANT PERSONS	EGO STRENGTH	PSYCHOSOCIAL MODALITIES	PSYCHOSEXUAL STAGES
1st Year Tilt Pos. I Neg.	BASIC TRUST vs. BASIC MISTRUST	MATERNAL PERSON	HOPE	TO GET / TO GIVE IN RETURN	ORAL-RESPIRATORY SENSORY-KINESTHETIC (INCORPORATIVE MODES)
Pos. II Neg.	AUTONOMY vs. SHAME, DOUBT	PARENTAL PERSON	WILL	TO HOLD ON / TO LET GO	ANAL-URETHRAL MUSCULAR (RETENTIVE-ELIMINATIVE)
Pos. III Neg.	INITIATIVE vs. GUILT	BASIC FAMILY	PURPOSE	TO MAKE (GO AFTER) / TO "MAKE LIKE" (PLAY)	INFANTILE-GENITAL LOCOMOTOR
Pos. IV Neg.	INDUSTRY vs. INFERIORITY	NEIGHBORHOOD, SCHOOL	COMPETENCE	TO MAKE THINGS (COMPLETING)	LATENCY
Pos. V Neg.	IDENTITY vs. IDENTITY DIFFUSION	PEER GROUPS; MODELS OF LEADERSHIP	FIDELITY	TO BE ONESELF (OR NOT BE) / TO SHARE BEING ONESELF	PUBERTY
Pos. VI Neg.	INTIMACY vs. ISOLATION	PARTNERS IN FRIENDSHIP, SEX, COMPETITION, COOPERATION	LOVE	TO LOSE AND FIND ONESELF IN ANOTHER	GENITALITY
Pos. VII Neg.	GENERATIVITY vs. STAGNATION	DIVIDED LABOR & SHARED HOUSEHOLD	CARE	TO MAKE BE / TO TAKE CARE OF	
Pos. VIII Neg.	INTEGRITY vs. DESPAIR	HUMANKIND	WISDOM	TO BE THROUGH HAVING BEEN / TO FACE "NOT BEING"	

Eric Erickson's Psycho-Social Graph

If one has developed positively in adolescence—which *can* be from ages fourteen to forty-four—then one can go on to intimacy, and mature and meaningful relationships, then onto Generativity and Integrity (wisdom) in old age. If, at the Identity Stage, one remains in the negative development, one will pass into old age with isolation, stagnation, and despair. The outline is easy to read, easy to follow, and easy to learn from (and print).

If you question adolescence being 14 to 44, then go back to the beginning of Erickson's explanation and as you read, you will notice that at the stage of Identity, if this is in the negative, you will have to return to step one and experience each step in the positive until you reach identity in the positive state. This takes time, and every individual is different. As in all things, there is no blanket, one time process, for everyone. Everyone has their own unique journey.

A journey that aligns with our chakra experiences.

For the sake of spiritual growth, learning the graph will give you additional insight for discernment and moral decision-making, and for understanding and identifying positive versus negative behavioral patterns. Understanding the human condition is the key to tolerance, acceptance of others, the ability to love others, and for personal growth.

Historical Graph: Global Trends

(influenced by universal and planetary shifts in a vast and expanding universe)

AGRICULTURAL AGE ▼	INDUSTRIAL AGE ▼	INFORMATION AGE ▼	AGE OF INTELLIGENCE
			Evolution goes Inward to Human conciousness
1800'S-1950	1930/40-1970'S	1970'S-1990'S	2000-? ? ?
Approx. 125 years	Approx. 50 years	Approx 20 years	Overlaps "Info Age"
to peak	to peak	to peak	Evolutionary— Unlimited Potential

Eras peak faster and faster. Major changes took twenty-five to fifty years and more; change now takes place in days, weeks, months. Eras overlap in the developmental stages. *Age of Intelligence (the New World Age), and Cosmic Consciousness (the next evolutionary age) are "Energy-based" Eras.*

Twenty-First Century—3rd Millennium
    Age of Aquarius = age of transcendence and wholeness★
      ★ Always a struggle, but now with greater knowledge and higher consciousness, and the impulse of an evolutionary force influencing all humanity.
    (The Twentieth Century = age of Pisces and Aries = age of wars and deeper human understanding.)

Certainty (what is)/Uncertainty (what isn't)

In the reality of change and possibility, nothing is as good as it will be. *Possibility equals "what isn't but could be."* Survival is having more of what already is, having things the way they have always been. Stagnation is when "what is" (present) becomes more important than "what isn't" (future). What you have already produced is no longer possible, therefore, no longer a priority of importance. There is always possibility in "what isn't"; producing results, one after the other, leads to success.

The need to be right is a need to "look good" (ego). A lack of neediness is open to possibility. *Possibility doesn't come out of need, but simply because it is possible.* If you want something, you have to bring it to the party! The spirit supports manifestation of possibilities—an unfolding of the new.

"What is" equals certainty (the comfort zone); "what isn't" equals uncertainty; an ongoing circle of possibilities for creating new realities. The journey is always more interesting than the arrival. The present equals "what is." "What isn't" equals the future and the past; we learn from history (past) how to create a better future. In summary:

Certainty = Box of limitations; the box is limiting/closed (the present). Uncertainty = Eternal Circle of POSSIBILITIES/open (the future)

Living In The Moment

Well, my friends, in reflecting on the contents of this book, so far, one word comes to mind that works well as an overall summary. That word is *emergence*. Life is like living in continual emergence! An emergence from one's past; from one's personal journey into this moment. This moment is about the emergence of "being," arrival in this time and place as spirit in human form. Since nothing is ever the same tomorrow as it is today, emergence is a moment-to-moment reality. Each moment is transformative when we acknowledge the truth that it bears. *What is not acknowledged cannot be transformed.*

When polarized in positions of "right and wrong," possibilities do not emerge; they pass you by. You have to do your soul work: transcend the ego and break through denial, traumas, and righteous attitudes. As in the chakras, one must forgive, heal, and transition through woundology and the fourth chakra (the heart chakra), surrendering to God's will. It is here where emergence of the Essential Code begins to embed into one's psyche and cultivate the soul.

One's journey transitions quickly when one shifts rapidly in beliefs and attitudes. Failure to successfully complete this process breaks the code! The *Essential Code* then becomes an ideal, versus a transformative and sacred way of being and living.

Every new insight, enlightenment, and experience compels another emerging reality. Every cosmic revelation bridges another emerging unknown. With every emergence comes the free will to create and co-create, to be fully alive with the Essential Code embedded in a quiet contentment of sacred and emerging truths. Truths that bubble up from within co-creative communities and global and cosmic masters, and vibrate in the souls of all humanity, saying, *"I am . . . a wave of love!"*

What a trip! To be the chosen people placed on earth during a great planetary and cosmic change; one that humans have never witnessed before, and the universe has not experienced in over 5,125 years, with a second cycle of 26,625 years, climaxing at the same time. As if this isn't enough, we are the trusted species to usher in a new world age of high-frequency vibrations at the same time. How awesome can it get!

Humanity has been given the choice of ushering in a peaceful and sacred new world age or allowing continued devastation. Of course, we choose a sacred and peaceful world, a destiny that compels a passionate response-ability as presented in the sacred words and messages of *the Essential Code*! There is an urgency to embody *the Essential Code* and to create a nurturing, co-creative synergy of communion amid communities in our global village. This will send a coded language of waves, connecting our sacred beliefs to the sacred energies of the universe. Gregg Braden explains, "we can tune our beliefs to preserve or destroy all that we cherish, including life itself." Humanity has the awesome opportunity of creating the future. The Mayan calendar ending in 2012 is the emergence of a new world age. What kind of a world will it be? We are living in a moment of uncertainty, a time of great possibilities. A time to put aside the old, the past, to move past what is (not much of "what is" is working anyway!) and co-create what is possible, *what has not yet been!*

Live in the moment, with all of your passion, *and embed the sacred code.*

The Essential Code incarnates a transcended ego with deep feelings of peace, love, forgiveness, appreciation, gratitude, and compassion. Then, bonding this indispensable essence within one's heart as one's sacred way of being and living. Swift embodiment of this sacred way of being, and co-creating new systems in a community of unity, is an urgency of all time!

To have the kind of world we want, we must first be the kind of person we want the world to be. Accelerate your evolutionary impulse. Infuse your life with joy and communion, embed an infinite "stretch," fulfill your highest purpose. Just do it!

Master your spirit by mastering the Code. Now is the moment to awaken to your divine magnificence and expand the sacred waves of your heart like never before! ♥

Our Soul Work

Do not second guess the spirit;
your lists of preferences
mean nothing.
Spirit is not interested in your comfort
but in breaking you apart
until your shell crumbles
and you are reborn as love.

(Poem by Tanis Helliwell from 'Embraced by Love)
Printed with author's permission

♥ *Visit The 'Essential Code' Web Pages* ♥

♥ *www.TheEssentialCode.com* ♥

PART IV

Stretching the Mind

"A mind stretched to a new idea never returns to original dimension."
—Dr. Wayne Dyer

Nothing and no one operates as a single cell. From the chaos at the beginning of our planet (a mini speck at birth) to the vast universe, everything is interconnected to everything else. When studying the cosmos, I learned that the principles of the universe apply to humanity and life on earth, even to our mundane daily lives. As above, so it is below! (*Canticle to the Cosmos,* Brian Swimme DVD)

Chaos Stands at the Door to Our Own Personal Growth

Just like the chaos in the birthing of our planet and the growth process that followed, when chaos is present in our daily lives, change follows. If there is repetitive chaos and no growth or initiating of change to a greater and better state of being, then beware: a stagnant situation exists. The question is, "What are you going to do about it?" Remember, you can only change *self,* no one else. What has to happen for you to live a healthier, happier, more loving lifestyle?

Every thought has energy. Are your thoughts about the other person or situation? Dwelling on what you don't want will create more of what you don't want! Are your thoughts on what you need to do to move your life forward? Can you love yourself enough to surrender and evolve out of the chaos and into a healthier being and the pursuit of happiness? Create your own inner evolutionary world with faith; surrender your fears. In nature's beauty, there is nothing that blooms to perfection without the toiling and nurturing of a caring universe, the caring hands of a loving presence. Be that presence!

You are a mini universe within; it is your caring hands and loving presence that will evolve your inner universe through a spiraling process of surrender to new growth and new experiences. Break through old patterns of being, and you will find that happiness *is* the way, rather than pursuing it. Breakthrough creates change, and when things change, everything tends to change. Be open, and stretch, stretch, stretch!

I have experienced this scenario of chaos at the threshold of change throughout my life. Once one recognizes this pattern, one has greater tolerance and inner knowing that the pot of gold at the end of the rainbow is just ahead. Patience, prayer, and God's grace sustains and strengthens the journey back to symmetry.

After years of efforts to create greater spiritual growth within the parish, I was guided by a kindred spirit, a friend and Catholic sister from St. Joseph's Order in Boston, to studies in cosmology and spirituality. The excitement and inner knowing that I was following my path to a mind-stretching adventure on one hand, and letting go of a dysfunctional status quo encircled by longtime friends and years of hard work on the other hand, created a huge transitional period.

As in "Our Soul Work" poem, I was broken apart as my mundane, incubated shell crumbled, *"and the day came, when the risk to remain tight in the bud was more painful than the risk it took to bloom" (quote by Anais Nin).*

Withdrawal from an institution that I had given over 100 percent was like the experience of any other loss. Withdrawal came in steps, and the healing process was sometimes painful. The duality of this pain/joy transition played out in my inner emotions. Transitioning into a more holistic faith also meant moving on in relationships, leaving people I cared about, while at the same time being confronted by the cold status quo (the "I told you so" mentality of those who were glad that I was no longer a thorn in their side). This is like what I've experienced before; when I gently announced plans to move on, the others (in this case, my opposition) couldn't believe I would be so foolish, and their conclusion that there was something wrong with me. Ahhh, so be it.

The ongoing transitions were a true test of my ego. Incarnating a transcended ego was the byproduct of my search for meaning. Yet, true healing could not be experienced until I not only instantaneously experienced forgiveness but also developed a deep compassion for the opposition I had encountered. Greater understanding through education and advancement in spiritual studies enabled an emergent sacredness for all that is. Gratitude swells in appreciation of the lessons, God's grace of strength, and an essence of elevated energy vibrations spiral within. Ambiguity smudged any possible clarity in regards to my destiny; I was simply flowing in awesome discovery and loving every moment.

In retrospect, my experiences were just what they needed to be for me to grow and to gain a greater trust and faith in the unknown—to transition from certainty to uncertainty, while learning that my inner pain was a call to greater inner growth. I could not blame my inner pain on what was happening outside of me. I had to own it, to seek understanding and greater insight. Which enabled healing revelations and peace within.

I came through much stronger—physically, emotionally, and spiritually. The inner experience met God through intuitive, and at times, even psychic connection; inner knowing evolved as I evolved in spirit. Words alone cannot adequately explain. I grew into a new and more profound state of being—a closer relationship with God. How awesome and unexplainable—

experiencing pain and elating joy . . . a progressive spiritual transition, for sure.

I transitioned from a stagnated environment to a turning point where I experienced environments of the deepest and most sacred energies. My heart pulsed with a new love, deep compassion, appreciation, and gratitude for all my wonderful blessings.

Earlier on, I had thought that I was flowing with everything. But now I know that I was really trying to control everything. I know this because I have since surrendered control to God's will. I can now experience the stage where life simply flows in discovery of what God has in store with a heartfelt love and gratitude. My journey has been intense, with lots of experiences. But I make the journey with trust that all is well, even when it seems otherwise. Coming to know God is not a pleasure trip; one's soul would never progress without the inner contemplation that comes from the experience of pain. The awesomeness of the journey creates a profound gratitude for the privilege of life on earth, the growth and connection to all that is, and our co-creative source. Earth School is a magnificent and mystical place where we all discover, learn, and grow into our spirit being!

Our gorgeous blue-and-green planet was created with just the right balance between all the chemicals. As previously stated, science informs us that the tiniest of difference in any one chemical at the chaos of the "big bang", and our world and humanity would not be here. This universal principle of divine balance affects all things. In the universe, nothing remains stagnant. There's either growth or decay and death. *Everything* requires balanced energies to flourish—the yin and yang of life, the male and female of creation. This is the cosmology and spirituality of all that is—the cosmic energy of past-present-future, balanced by earth's collective synergy of love and harmony, enabling the evolutionary shift now in process; "as above, it is below." These energies radiate from our higher self and embodiment of the *Essential Code*. Now is the time! Each person is valued and uniquely precious and valuable.

The Age of Intelligence

Recent quantum physics and revealing insights from science indicate that school textbooks are now obsolete. The Age of Intelligence is constantly unfolding greater human consciousness. Cutting-edge insight is rapidly being revealed to us from all spokes of the wheel—the masters of various areas of life, research, and intelligence—resulting in greater collective insight and understanding of truths. Connections have manifested between ancient spiritual writings and the discoveries and the intelligence of today. All of this is happening within a short period of time.

In the birth of a new world age, perhaps the Age of Cosmic Consciousness is next? (*Reference: Historical Graph of Global Trends*)

Astological Cycles

The Mayan calendar was once interpreted as the end of the world. However, we now know that it depicts the end of astrological cycles. Science has discovered cosmic cycles layered within larger cycles, with a vast time lapse in years. No one experiences these, except if he happens to be on Earth at the time that the cycles end—e.g., the Mayan calendar calculates until the year 2012, when it ends a 5,125-year cycle, along with a 26,625 year cycle that it takes for the earth to experience one complete wobble. These cycles affect our cycles of weather, global warming, loss of species, and more.

Cycles operate in all areas of daily life: our calendar, weather, astrology, the economy, etc. How many can you list? Since we were not around at the beginning of long-term cosmic cycles, we are only aware of them—and their effect on the world and our lives—through the revelations of quantum science and the ongoing research into science and spirituality. The luminary masters of our day are intuitively evolving and bringing us more in-depth knowledge and spiritual consciousness. Knowledge simply exists everywhere, all at once, like waves of energy flowing through the universe. The energy and intuitive minds of luminaries and quantum science can often "tune in" to waves of universal knowledge from anywhere and everywhere. Their co-creative minds deeply engage in the mystery and riddles of the universe.

The Cutting Edge

For you and me to advance in cutting-edge knowledge, one has to be a seeker and devour the publications of those on the cutting edge of breaking research. There is an abundance of highly intelligent knowledge available—knowledge you will not find on your television or in the mass media. The profound results will stretch the mind to a place from which there is no return. Certainly, there is more cutting-edge science and evolutionary insight to be found on YouTube than in the media. You need only enter the subject matter. Expanding the mind in this manner awakens one's creative potential, allowing the spirit self to formulate and connect the vastness of God's infinite truths in an ongoing new and collective awareness.

Simple Cosmology

The old cosmology said, "Worship the Creator, not the creation." But times are different now. "If we don't worship the Creator in and through creation, our worship will lead to death rather than life."

Another difference between these cosmologies is the way each understands the organization of creation. The first diagram is an example of what is sometimes referred to as the Western hierarchy of values. The second diagram is our true integral community.

The Old Cosmology

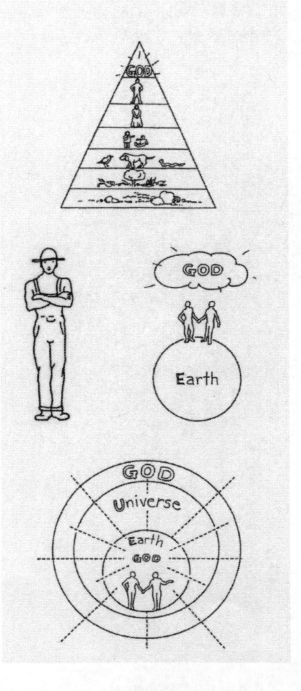

The New Cosmology

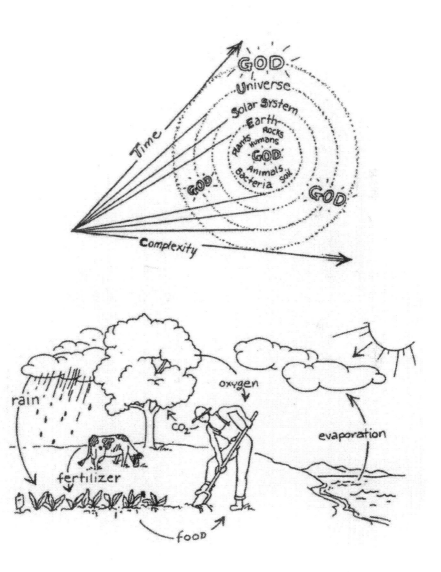

The new cosmology understands that everything is changing, that we are part of a time-development universe. As time continues, creation becomes more complex and more capable of realizing its inner spiritual potential. In other words, the universe is maturing. Finally, it makes a world of difference, literally, how we perceive an individual human being in our imagination. From the old perspective, a farmer might be imagined as something like the single man (the old cosmology). This illustration is a misleading abstraction. There is no such thing as an isolated human being—except in our imagination. Any human in actual existence exists *only* as a member of the wider community of life, air, water, and soil. To think of ourselves as separate from the rest of nature as we have may have been important for our evolutionary development. To continue seeing ourselves this way any longer, however, is suicidal. The new cosmology is a truer depiction of a farmer.

Our true condition is that we are each an integral member of the entire life community. What we do to the earth, we do to ourselves. On the following page is a pledge that I wrote in 1993, incorporating the new cosmology in its true form, and as we know it today.

PLEDGE TO THE UNIVERSE

I / WE PLEDGE
   To Honor Oneness of the Universe
   Bonding of All Creation
   Interconnected Life, Earth, Air
   Fire and Sun, Water and Sea.

I / WE PLEDGE
   To Seek Understanding and Forgiveness
   Compassion and Coherence
   Integrity, Justice, Peace
   New Wisdom and Unity.

I / WE PLEDGE
   To Co-Creatively Generate
   A Humane and Sustainable Community
   Truth, Love, Beauty, of the Universe and Soul
   Earth, Humans, and all Life
   As One Interwoven, Sacred Whole.

   ~ Arvetta Souza
   ~ 1993 ~

Cosmic Cycles

Science and research informs us of the end of a 26,625-year cosmic cycle and the end of the Mayan calendar, indicating changes taking place that are beyond the average person's knowledge, and scientists are still researching. Currently, there is a lowering of the earth's magnetic field and changes in weather patterns. The magnetic field guards our planet and guides our creatures. What the cosmic changes mean for the future is up to mankind. The efforts of humanity to avoid adding to global warming and to create peace, compassion, and new and sustainable systems are urgent steps for mankind.

Science also states that low magnetic fields present conditions for easier transitions in beliefs and greater holistic insight. For those who can accept change, adjustments will be easier, and those who resist or are unable to change will find life stressful and more difficult.

All considered several energies are peaking at the same time: the December 21, 2012 solstice, cosmic, earth, and human evolutionary energies. All connected energies will be affected in some way. Our thoughts, emotions, and beliefs all affect the way we experience change. By altering the way we think and feel about change, we can actually transition more easily. The following elements all suggest that, with heartfelt efforts, we can create the kind of destiny we dream of: a collective view of essential energies throughout the cosmological, spiritual, and global trends, and our current era of intelligence, astrological cycles, higher frequency in personal development, and the holistic values of conscious evolution. Our feelings of love, appreciation, gratitude, and care—not just thoughts but heartfelt *feelings*—can create a norm of cooperation, healing, and peace. We can collectively determine the kind of world we live in! Change can take place instantly or gradually. The kind of collective synergy waves humanity sends forth will likely determine the duration and intensity of man's experience. Earth's inhabitants are experiencing a huge first in the history of all mankind, the birthing of a new world age. It is a cosmic event demanding non-violence and loving, co-creative, communities of communion embedded in our global village and the co-creation of environments of justice in local and global systems.

"We need to continually remind ourselves that to have the type of world we want, we first must be the kind of person we want the world and others to be, always seeking a greater depth in the embodiment of the Essential Code, the code and loving path to our sacred destiny."

~ ARVETTA M. SOUZA

♥ Further information: *www.TheEssentialCode.com* ♥

The TIME TO CHOOSE . . . Is NOW

**A human being is
a part of the whole, called
by us the *universe,* a part limited in
time and space. He experiences himself—his
thoughts and feelings as something separated
from the rest . . . a kind of optical delusion
of his consciousness. This delusion is a
kind of prison for us, restricting us to our
personal desires and to affection for a few
persons nearest to us. Our task must be to
free ourselves from this prison by widening
our circle of compassion to embrace
all living creatures and the
whole of nature in its
beauty.**

~ ALBERT EINSTEIN

Left-Brain—Right-Brain Hemispheres

The left—and right-brain activity is an interesting part of understanding the human response. The left brain is our logical, rational, "concrete" side. Mathematical ability and reasoning, language and scientific skills are located in the left brain. Men tend to be more left-brain active than women. It is possible that the new spiritual energy coming from the cosmos is also affecting the male aspects in such a way that more men are responding from the spiritual, intuitive, right-brain side than ever before. Welcome, guys! You have been missed!

Women tend to respond more readily from the right brain, as textbooks tell us, because women tend to be more compassionate. Women's intuition has always been a noted trait. Other skills of the right brain include spirituality, imagination, creativity, art, and insight. In a high-tech world, with women in careers and other avenues of personal development, many women today respond just as readily from the left brain as do males. However, women still tend to respond in greater numbers than men from the spiritual and intuitive aspects of the brain.

One can be of a high intellect but be devoid of spiritual and intuitive insight. *One cannot reach the spiritual from one's intellect.* You will often find a spiritual person who is not in the intellectual mode of life. The spiritual and the intellectual are two different energies and develop from different parts of the brain. Reaching the spiritual is a matter of a soulful and open mind, and a heartfelt desire to know God—devoid of attachment to the ego, judgment, or the rational. The spirit life is not a matter of reasoning; it is an intuitive inner knowing, a God-centered energy and wisdom. (Both are intangibles.) This is different from religion. Organized religion has dogma—laws and rules of behavior and denominational identity. The spirit cannot be boxed in, so neither is growth in spiritual consciousness and intuition (God's silent inner voice).

To gain a better insight into the workings of the two sides of the brain, refer to the human energy system as explained through the energies of the chakras. You can track the unfolding of spirit life through the developmental aspects of the chakra energies, and visually see where blocked energies can actually prevent one from experiencing a deeper and more profound connection to the divine (right-brain function). The chakras are a spiraling, evolving process.

By experiencing the above inventory process, one can easily come to understand how crucial it is to nourish personal development from the cradle through early childhood, adolescence, and adulthood. Inner growth and ongoing personal development are an ongoing lifetime experience.

Heart-filled love and the challenging of both sides of the brain at all ages of development is crucial to elevating one's experiences of life, the universe, and the divine. To manifest anything, we need both sides of the brain. To sustain a lifetime of spiritual growth is to transcend egoic patterns, to endlessly seek to evolve with greater consciousness. The most dreamed-of state of being—a depth, breadth, joyous gratitude, peace, and awesomeness of spirit—evolves to a level where dualities fade away and an unfolding oneness becomes embedded in our soul. All is one, the *Essential Code* incarnate.

"An educated conscience is priceless," in this space and time, is definitely applicable. To prepare for the future, one needs a discernment of history and the now. The brain is a very delicate instrument. Repetitive patterns become embedded habits that can arrest one's growth. The kind of stimulation the brain receives is either life-supporting or life-denying. The Information Age of the past two to three decades has changed the way our youth use their time. Technology (information) peaked in a very short period of time; our teens now spend their time interacting with machines instead of with other people.

In youth ministry, the saying goes, "High-tech demands high-touch,"—a high quality of one-on-one time with people. I have found this to be true. Youth who spend most of their time with technology tend to be lacking empathy. Two decades of this pattern and we have a collective body of emotionally confused youth, devoid of respectful human interactive and relational skills. There is a void that they fill with sex, drugs, drinking, and wild parties. Most work hard but sustain a simplistic black-and-white lifestyle of study hard, play hard (so as not to talk, think, or feel in regards to life and true reality). Many of these youth experience these same patterns in their homes. There is little respect for the earth, people or things, feelings, or good manners.

The result is that our average youth is losing the ability to feel compassion. They've become inept in building meaningfulness; they've lost the right-brain vibes required for healthy whole-brain balance. Assertiveness becomes extreme as bully or toughness; the youths bully to avoid being seen by their peers as weak or sensitive, and maybe from an unconscious, recessed anger due to the missing elements in their lives.

Youths who are addicted to video games and media that glorify violence and a lack of value for life are desperately in need of a personal transition to find the values that enable adequate energies, emotions, and leadership skills. These positive values are necessary for successful participation and leadership in the new world that they will inherit. A society lacking in empathy and compassion is not only dangerous to the inhabitants, but is an unsustainable pattern.

Isn't it noticeable that being entertained is of higher priority to our American youth than the youth of other countries. How many countries are rising above America's numbers in college grads, masters, PhDs, and highly trained leaders of their fields? What has happened to our family structure that demanded high standards in principles, values, honesty, and human decency and respect? What has happened to the traits that build a foundation for healthy brain development? Where is the circle of warmth that nourishes our youth and our families—co-creating a connective sense of belonging?

Freedom is not free; it is not doing what you want, it is earned. Freedom demands accountability and heart-based responsibility! It seems a rapid and radical shift is in order regarding daily lifestyles, educational patterns, institutional awareness, and an overall concern for the sacredness of humanity and our planet as a whole. It all begins in the *brain, and unfolds through the heart!*

We need to re-invent ourselves and how we relate to each other, our home, planet Earth, and the universe as a divine whole. The age of wild consumption is past. Our materialistic world has been more concerned with left-brain intelligence than in developing right-brain power. This is a shift that has to come from every home, office, corporate, institutional and political entity, and should have started yesterday!

The world has always measured success by materialistic means: money, ownership, and *things* (left brain). However, *the universe measures success by how much you have learned.* The transcendence of the ego, a balanced brain, wisdom, and an eternal, evolving consciousness are all energies of the upper chakras; it takes conscious effort and human desire to grow, to prepare for the opportunity of a coherent future. Today's structures will not be sustainable in the new world age. Many lost jobs will not return. We are already into the transition—the chaos stage of change is here, now, exploding all around us.

A Written Exercise—Forming Goals for Change

I have learned that the questions to ask are: **1)** What do you want? Then describe, in the clearest detail possible, what that is. (Write it down, be complete!) **2)** What do you have to do to get there? Answer by beginning where you are now, and explain in detail all that you will need to do or change in order to make it happen. **3)** Once you have reached your goal, what will it look like? Describe in detail everything that will be happening and your feelings, as well as the place that you will personally be in. Make it vivid! Once this is completed in every detail, the next question is: What do I have to do to make it happen? You now have a vision of the "end." Go backward and list the step-by-step process you need to take until you get back to the beginning, and step one is clarified. Then just do it . . . step-by-step, always with your vision clearly in your mind, and with patience, determination, love, and faith.

Note: There is a difference between #2 and the last question. In #2, you are listing the changes you will have to enact to make what you want materialize. The last question takes in the bird's-eye view of the whole mental picture of re-inventing yourself and your circumstances, to find the first step to the last in doing so.

Once the journey begins, look for coincidences and synchronicities along the way. They are awesome and a sure sign that the spirit is working with you. As previously stated, the spirit always supports efforts toward a higher frequency of being.

Ref: Three-Step Process: Dr. Richard Bandler's Techniques for Therapy—

> - for resolving relationship problems (both have to participate);
> - for goal-setting in most situations.

Whole Brain Diagram with
Right and Left Brain Functions

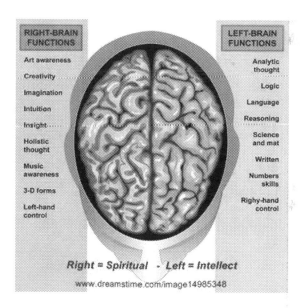

PART V

Expanded Perceptions

"When we truly believe in a perception, we see it as the one and only reality and ignore all other possible realities."
"Spontaneous Evolution"
—Bruce H. Lipton, PhD and Steve Bhaerman

Perception flows from the five senses and connects us to the external world. Expanded perception flows from the higher frequency of spiritual energies, our inner world, and connects one to the energies of the upper chakras. (Perception is free of ego, judgment, and emotion.) As one evolves into a higher frequency of spiritual energy, expanded depths of perception flow into consciousness.

Science teaches us that everything is a form of energy. We can understand our body's energy system through the chakra centers. The chakras run vertically, aligned with the spine line of the body; a holographic system versus linear. Chakras are interrelated; everything relates to everything else. Understanding the energy of our anatomy, through the power of the human spirit, gives one "personal power"; this is contrary to external power, as seen in the world.

The chakras are our evolution of empowerment. When you obtain a sense of self (owning your chakras), you will be able to protect your energy from the addictive symbols of power—money, sex, prestige, etc. One could then expand one's intuitive abilities, synchronicities, and experiences of energy fields beyond the material world. Through our personal power, responsibility for our health is in our own hands. When you understand the seven energy centers (chakras) of your body, and how they regulate the flow of one's energy, you can avoid being controlled by your own "attachments" and the negative energy of others.

As Caroline Myss so clearly and accurately teaches, "Your biography becomes your biology." I highly recommend her book, *Anatomy of the Spirit, Harmony House, 1996.*

The following is a simple outline of the chakras for your convenience. A *simple outline is definitely inadequate.* The experiences stated in this book are meant to inspire you to seek further insight. I urge you to acquire the above-referenced book in order to obtain a full description and insight into chakra energies and the health issues involved with each chakra. I prefer Caroline's chakra teachings because of her combined spiritual and intuitive medical wisdom.

The seven centers are seven different levels of being, encompassing the areas of the body energized by each chakra and the emotions and health issues involved in each energy center. Healing the energy centers (chakras) frees the soul.

Negative experiences block chakra energy in the particular energy field that is involved. Your inner world awaits further discovery!

The Seven Chakra Centers

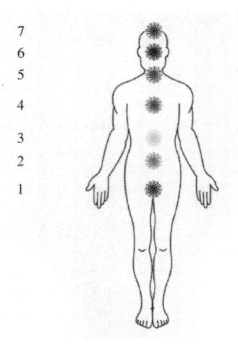

First Chakra: (Base Root—Survival)

Located at the base of the spine, this center relates to the will for survival; issues of work, money, family of origin; other groups; belonging; and safety. (Family of origin is the first group we let go of to move on in our growth; a repetitive scenario experienced as we travel the spiritual journey.

Second Chakra: (Relationships)

This is located just below the navel. This center relates to emotions, sex, power seeking attitude; flight-or-flee, materialism, authority and control, ownership, and addictions. Blocked energy can result in a lack of sexual and emotional boundaries. Instability keeps adrenaline flowing with fight-or-flight continually alert;

this prolonged stress can produce negative health issues. We seek out those who hold the same sense of right and wrong, disqualifying them if they change. Seeking vengeance is a highly toxic emotional poison that affects one's biological system.

Third Chakra: (Ego, the Mind and "Mind Games")

Located just below the ribs—third chakra relates to reasoning and logical thinking; to how much energy you have and how you use it; self-empowerment and the need to control others. One begins to separate from group thought. This is *the seat of your ego*: who you *think* you are, and your self-esteem. If energy is blocked, your energy will be low. The playing of power games and "woundology" resides here, refusing to allow birthing of your authentic self. The challenge is self-understanding, independence, and self-respect; holding on to past emotional wounds prevents spiritual advancement. Healing of wounds need not be long—it can be short and rapid, if you believe that it can. *Too often one lives with emotional perceptions, rather than forgiving, healing, and gaining healthy perspectives.*

Fourth Chakra: (Heart, selfless love, the gateway upward)

Located at the center of chest—plays an important role in relationships, as it represents universal, selfless love and expressions; relates to love, peace, your self-worth (how one values self). If energy is blocked, you lose touch with what you love and you are unforgiving of self and others. Sharing of emotional wounds is used as the substance and glue that binds relationships. The challenge is to heal, to form an empowered heart—to love, to seek health and healing (requires both physical and emotional healing), to move beyond self. Imbalance leads to exaggerated self-importance, possessiveness, selfishness; heart and immune-related disorders (e.g., cancer and AIDS).

Fifth Chakra: (Throat, will, communication, healing of wounds)

Located at the base of the throat (neck area). This center relates to self-expression, communication, psychic, and telepathy. The power of will: personal versus God's will. (Do you try to control the very guidance you are seeking?) Fear lets go to faith; we gain ability to make symbolic connection. Blocked energy results in poor communications; most common is loss of one's voice and confusion from the voices of others. Verbalizing of "wounds" is used to influence and control others; recessed fear of being exposed. Healing and forgiveness frees the soul from the need for personal vengeance, and perceiving self as a victim.

Sixth Chakra: ("Third eye," sixth sense, universal intelligence)

Located at the center of the forehead—relates to intuition and clairvoyance; discernment of truth, *to see as spirit*, to understand energy and holistic views, non-judgmental. An ability to release the old and embrace the new—to see that all things begin and end at the appropriate time. You gain ability for detachment, and no one person or group can determine your life's path. Blocked energy results in being blind to the truth, limited and judgmental thinking, intellectualizing. To become conscious is a process of letting go of illusion, defensiveness, and living in the past. Fear creates inertia and non-acceptance of the new, creating indecisiveness.

Seventh Chakra (Crown, beyond the elements and senses, and mundane transcendence

Located at the top of the head—the crown and spiritual connector—a knowingness—"to be still and know the truth." Our spirit knows things beyond what our mind could know. Intuition and inspiration, creation, and "all that is" reside here.

All is one. When energy is blocked, we are disconnected from a higher truth, we look for external answers (instead of listening to the inner voice within or an inner knowing from within). This chakra is the energy connection to the physical body—the entry point for human life force from supreme consciousness, the universe, and radiates to all energy centers and an earthly grounding. A spiritual state that transcends mundane realities, experiences the attainment of enlightenment.

♥ ♥ ♥

"Each choice we make, we either become more involved in the illusions of the physical world, or we invest energy into the power of spirit!"
—Caroline Myss, Anatomy of the Spirit, Harmony House, 1996

All seven chakras represent a different version of this one *essential lesson*. Every time we enhance our spirit, we strengthen our energy, and the stronger our energy field, the less we will connect to negative people and experiences. It is our task to give our best energy to every situation, with the understanding that we influence, but do not control, what we will experience tomorrow. No *thing* or person will be exactly the same tomorrow. Change is forever constant!

It's not an easy journey, processing through the chakras. But what is easy and what is just or healthy is seldom the same thing. When I experience negative aspects and feel resistance, I know it is time to reflect on where my energies are directed. The chakras are an honest and accurate guide. I trust the little voice within, and it informs me when I am out of balance.

I have deep gratitude for the expertise and intuitive talents of Caroline Myss; she is always discovering new panoramic views and then sharing them with the world. Her unique knowledge and ability as a spiritual teacher and medical intuitive blows me away! I gained my insight and ability in reading my energy from her. I extend a *huge* thank-you and lots of love to Caroline.

Unfolding Cycles

New beginnings often follow closures. Sometimes they overlap, spiraling onward and upward in the transition. Sometimes there is a space-pause in between, a lull of ambiguity. This lull is our opportunity to influence change in the direction of our choice. Either way, the embryo of our next lesson is birthing. Either passively, or when one actively chooses, only the ease and format of our lesson will vary.

Everything one has done in the past prepares one for what one will experience next. Our free will influences the *how,* but the *what,* is God's plan for us. Sometimes we experience the same result over and over again until we learn our lesson. Then, in doing so, we break the repetitive cycle and make better choices. An awareness of your cycles can create greater clarity in making decisions.

I have evolved to where I find life a pure joy! Words are inadequate in explaining my sincere and deep gratitude for the lessons learned and the consciousness gained. It has been an awesome lifetime, and it is still unfolding! Sharing experiences of my chakra energies, and the lessons learned, will perhaps give you greater insight into their energy centers. The greater insight you have the quicker and easier you can guide, and read, your own energies. We continually cycle through the chakras all of our life; they provide a spiraling map of our spiritual journey.

Life Experiences and the Chakras

I was first introduced to the chakras through spiritual venues, but the chakras didn't resonate. However, clarity came at a time when I was seeking greater understanding, this time directed toward healing the result of long time exposure to an emotionally charged environment.

In 1996, I was able to associate my illness, an inner-ear virus and the extended term of dizziness I endured, with real-life experiences that ended just prior to the onset of my illness in 1993, when my "biography became my biology". The most hellish year I have ever experienced had just ended. Nearly every effort extended as coordinator of a junior and high school level religious education program was met with opposition from the secretary. It was an environment of "crazy-making," to quote John Bradshaw's description of dysfunctional, controlling, and polarized behavior patterns.

Working from the same office and with less than a year in service, the newly hired youth minister found counseling a necessary part of his sanity, from which he was advised, and did, find work elsewhere. We were both considered deviant because we were working to co-create growth and greater spiritual experiences for all parishioners.

The status quo was a small, embedded and stagnated group who rejected everything representing growth. The members of this group had the impression that only they knew what was best for everyone, and what was best for everyone was what was comfortable for them. And, of course, what was comfortable for them was more of the same, more of what had always been. Sometimes they would try to revive outdated programs that had previously failed, or died out. Youth ministry to them was just "fun and games and inappropriate." There is no peaceful essence of the spirit in a polarized, control-oriented environment.

Working in the environment of the religious education office was an arena of dizzy "crazy-making" with a seesaw of emotional personalities. I saw the year through with no administrative support. There was no administrative desire to fire or even speak to the "secretary from hell," as referenced by neighboring parishes, and known by the archdiocesan office. This whirlwind was so unbelievable for any church, especially one with over a thousand students of the faith.

Looking back, I was determined not to quit. I felt strongly about keeping my commitment to the people, and to myself, it was a part of my integrity—of who I was. Even though my insight and understanding of their developmental behavior patterns created great tolerance and spontaneous forgiveness, at that time in my life I had no realization of my tolerance zone, or how long term, negative stress would affect my health.

Nine months of the dizzy, crazy-making patterns and my "biography became my biology." I suddenly experienced labyrinthitis, an inner-ear virus causing a dizzying vertigo that sent the world spinning like a top; I dared not open my eyes. The dizziness diminished very slowly, taking seven years to heal. In my search for healing, I researched several publications and healing techniques and finally paid a visit to Massachusetts Eye and Ear Hospital. I was told that the dizziness would eventually go away, but I would have to be patient. (That was at the three-year mark!)

I found that periods of concentration helped, so I focused on further education. With the extended periods of concentration, along with a diet devoid of stimulants—no caffeine, alcohol, chocolate, and wheat, healing gradually came. To this day, I cannot tolerate caffeine or alcohol. I have heard Dr. Wayne Dyer state, "There comes a time in the spiritual journey when you will simply not want these mind-altering substances in your body."

Wow, did God prepare me in advance?

The chakras have been a treasure in my life since learning about their energy centers in 1996. I believe there are no accidents! When you feel called by God, be aware, a transition is coming. This experience compelled me to move beyond dogmas of organized religion into a greater spiritual journey of cosmology and conscious evolution.

As you read through the chakras below, see if you can find the energies of the environment and experiences in this story. (Hint: Blocked energies of chakras One to Four; when trust is limited to a small group versus an open and secure trust in life itself, the chakra energies are blocked. Negative energies indicate blockage in the Chakra of which the energy applies. Transitional growth and healing is needed.)

CHAKRA 1:

The first chakra energy is referred to as the "tribal zone." This is the first energy of life and pertains to one's family of origin, one's sense of belonging, one's job, money matters, and safety issues. This is where we learn our first belief system and gain a sense of security and trust. (Money problems will often bring lower back pain, located directly behind the first chakra!) It also pertains to group(s) and belongingness. Your first group is your family of origin, but it also pertains to other groups that you become a part of. Groups tend to influence our way of thinking and being in the world.

When members grow and leave the family of origin, it is often a difficult change for the family. They feel there is something wrong with the person who is leaving, when actually the need for growth demands change. This same experience surfaces when leaving any group setting that you have outgrown. This is the chaos that stands at the threshold of change. Transitions leave one stronger, with greater self-authenticity.

I experienced the results of leaving outgrown boundaries all of my life. Developing your authentic self gives one the strength to honor the true self, regardless what, and always with heart filled love.

CHAKRA 2:

The second chakra is in regard to materialism, ownership, authority, and control issues. ("Keeping up with the Joneses," the ego trips—a familiar pattern?) Addiction is a big issue concerning the second chakra. Addiction can involve something otherwise considered to be good for you: exercise, religion, work, technology, sports, another person, etc. What makes anything an addiction? *Any unchanging behavior pattern motivated by the fear of internal growth. (Can't let go to grow!)*

We are familiar with the addiction to sex, alcohol, cigarettes, and drugs, all of which stagnate personal and spiritual growth. It is easy to become addicted. It takes a committed effort to withdraw and choose to create a balanced and healthy lifestyle. (Think about what motivates you—and *why.*)

Discovering my control issues was a wakeup call. It took time to let go of control. For me, it was part of a security that turned to trust as I realized God was in control *all* the time. All I had to do was relax and flow! It became an awesome experience discovering what was next, in total trust that the result would bring new and needed experiences. Sometimes the changes were difficult or ambiguous.

My simple desires have always been time with my family and friends, a comfortable home (rented or owned, it didn't matter), a balanced life, opportunities to use my abilities in service to others, and to continually learn and evolve in spiritual consciousness.

Addictions were certainly among my challenges. I won't go into boring detail. I will only tell you that my addictions differed with age, and two of them involved painful withdrawals. In retrospect, I now know that each one was part of my journey of personal growth, and once healed, the process had elevated my spiritual path. I still take inventory when trials appear in life, reflecting on what's happening, where I am in regards to spiritual aspects, and questioning a possible move toward a conscious shift. Letting go and moving on has always been the better decision! It's not easy, but gratitude has become an ongoing virtue as the mystery of life unfolds. Trusting in the Source became my ultimate path to peace. The mystery keeps life interesting, and discovery along the path is awesome!

Just as the universe has a woven web that covers everything—a divine matrix—human life is a mirror of that. A web of skin encompasses the body, spirit, and soul, creating a little universe within, unfolding in its mystery. "As above, so it is below."

CHAKRA 3:

The third chakra houses self-esteem and personal power energies. I experienced this chakra by learning to let go of the need for security and comfort; trying to control events blocked my own intuitive guidance. (One's intuitive guidance, by its nature, will direct one into new cycles of learning.) Letting go of the familiar, what seems to be secure and certain, allowing the uncertain to unfold and manifest, is God's ongoing plan for all of us. Self-esteem, faith that all is well, and trust in God and life itself is not always an easy way of experiencing daily life. But it is the spiritual path. As soon as an issue is resolved, another appears. How else is the development of human/spiritual potential possible? As Caroline Myss writes, "Because we are often driven with personal conflicts, we need the spiritual challenge of 'becoming empty in order to be made full,' to die to old habits and self-images in order to be reborn, with great trepidation." (*Anatomy of the Spirit*) *This is a* necessary transition for moving from ego to the inner sanctuary, where we can respond to life from divine essence.

This brings to mind what a Ministry retreat referred to as "the Easter weekends of life." *Good Fridays are the times we are nailed to the cross (when we acquire our wounds and hurts, etc.); Holy Saturdays are a time to work through the issues,* process them, pray for guidance, to understand, forgive, heal and grow; *Easter Sundays are the time to rejoice in* heart-filled love, gratitude, praise, and glory, and move on to a healthier pattern of being. We all experience Easter weekends of life—we vary in the time it takes to reach Easter Sunday. Not to do so is to refuse to grow, creating stagnated energy, blocking of the chakras, and preventing ongoing spiritual enlightenment.

Creating chaos can also be an addiction. The quiet is unfamiliar, and therefore, uncomfortable. And so, unconsciously, one creates chaos to feel alive in what is familiar—a psyche "high" and attention-getter. Healing can take place with the help of a holistic therapist. Whether it is a lengthy or short period of therapy depends on what the person *believes* it can be! This transition is a "journey to the heart."

People who cannot let go of their wounds become wound addicts. The question to ask and honestly respond to is: "Are you really happy in your life? If not, what are you doing to change it?" Ask "What do I have to let go of?" In my journey, I have had to let go of many things: people I love, places I love, addictions, control issues, my sense of security, a sense of belonging, a belief system that no longer served my spirit, people I considered to be friends, my youngest son, and reconciliation with loved ones who continually and persistently choose to live in compelling woundology and vengeful control. These are the major events, but minor events happen every day to challenge what we believe to be truth. (Many things can be true, but at the root of all we see as true is the truth of our frequency of spirit—our essence in vibration. Our journey is self-revealing!

No one obtains meaningful growth by living a misty and blissful life. New cycles of learning are sometimes uncomfortable, as is separating from group thought. To thrust forward is to choose the path of few footprints, with faith and no guarantees—evolving one's trust, with perseverance, insight, and foresight.

The first three chakras involve love in the external world. Building self-esteem is self-love and an internal challenge. Transcending the ego is a big one! Scripture refers to this as "dying to self and being born again." A transcendence. I was able to move into change by recognizing the overwhelming presence of ego in others. Taking inventory of my thoughts and actions in regard to the ego was a real eye-opening experience. Ego is good for egging one on (to complete what one has started). Profound spiritual insight can transcend a controlling ego with gratitude, humility (root meaning—"truth"), and an inner path filled with divine love. Dr. Wayne Dyer says, "Ego is 'edging God out!'"

CHAKRA 4:

The fourth chakra houses our emotional power—our emotional development. The fourth chakra is the heart chakra. This is our most powerful energy; it is where love resides, and is our *strongest energy-vibrating organ*. Our heartfelt love vibrates ripples of energy that flow out to, and are sustainable by, the universe. Our relationships are guided by a divine plan. Every encounter has a reason and a purpose in our life—we learn by interacting with other people; we learn the importance of healthy self-esteem and opportunities for affirming it.

It was not easy developing and sustaining a sense of who I am in the midst of drama and chaos, and indicative, verbal accusations that something was wrong with me. I have been labeled as being the cause of others' problems, that the behaviors of others were my fault. It is easier to blame others than to grow and become self-accountable.

For me, surviving the blame game required healing, high self-esteem, a transcended ego, soulful wisdom, and a deep gratitude for an abundance of God's grace and spontaneous understanding of behavior patterns.

It was a long journey before I finally arrived at a place where I understood that my life was just where it was meant to be—before I surrendered to the Divine Source. Letting go does not mean being irresponsible and passive. It does mean letting go of control and attachment to outcomes. I discovered that I was on my purpose in life—that our purpose is always to learn in order to further the soul-growth of self and others.

Sometimes the lesson was for me. Sometimes I was the teacher or catalyst for the lessons that others came to Earth School to learn. Responsibility for their learning and attitude is not in my realm, but abstaining from the victim role and sustaining my integrity is. Sometimes this was accomplished by letting go, silently sending love and blessing to others, and moving on. It is impossible to be a responsible participant in life without chaos and finding that there are people in this world who simply do not like you, for whatever known or unknown reason.

Love energies are life's greatest power and always at the core of life crises. The love of self elevates energies, enabling one to move beyond the tribal patterns of the lower chakras, to leave behind unproductive patterns, and to enter into the lessons of our heart center. It is in possessing a strong understanding of self that enables one to heal, to avoid role-playing, and to be open to serve in a meaningful way. The male/female roles have evolved into a partnership of shared responsibilities. To know who one is, to feel secure in who you are, to participate in the moment without ego reservation are energies of today. There is higher potential for success and intimacy between two people who have a true understanding of who they are.

In gaining a sense of self, you cannot continue to live in your past, locked into childhood wounds. Self-love means caring for one's self enough to forgive the people you hold responsible for wounds, so wounds can no longer cause damage. Wounds do nothing to others; they can only damage you.

Forgiveness is no longer seen as an option. It is now understood as a necessary path to healing. Forgiveness is a spiritual act, a right-brain function. Forgiveness opens oneself to the heart-centered healing power of love. *Inner wounds keep one living in the past and keep one from evolving in spiritual consciousness.* **Spirituality, a right-brain function, cannot be reached through the intellect, a left-brain function.** Only through heart energy can one heal, and only by working through the challenges of the heart chakra does one evolve in spiritual consciousness. How can one advance in spiritual consciousness and still hold on to repressed anger and unresolved wounds (Dr. Bradshaw's *"wounded inner child"*)?

This is much like India's "oneness blessing," which can only be received by those who have prepared by healing all hurts, whose energy has been cleared of tribal and emotional wounds, and whose hearts are centered on unconditional love, compassion, gratitude, and service to others.

Woundology and status quo groups operate from the same frequency level. Both are energies of the first three chakras. Wounds become the glue that binds relationships together, creating wound addicts. Healing demands the healing of these wounds, and resolving and healing of group addiction. If one member of the group heals and the others do not, then healing demands letting go of the group and moving on, finding a healthier and higher self-loving way of being. Breaking an addiction is not easy, but it is our salvation and the passage through the heart chakra. Passage through the heart chakra prepares us for evolving in our spiritual frequency. Allowing wounds to control one's life weighs heavily on one's respect and ability to grow. Role-playing presents a false self, and deep soulful meaning is unattainable due to the lack of an empowered heart and self-empowered love. The empty hole within cannot be gratified. Below are excerpts from *Anatomy of the Spirit* (Caroline Myss) for your reflection.

- ♥ "Forgiveness is an act of consciousness. One that liberates the soul from the need for personal vengeance and the perception of oneself as a victim." (215)
- ♥ "Everything in and about our lives runs off the fuel of our hearts. We will all have experiences meant to 'break our hearts'—not in half, but wide open!" (216)
- ♥ "The only path toward spiritual consciousness is through the heart. One must work their way through the heart Chakra to evolve in the upper chakras." (217)

I wish that I had chakra knowledge years earlier! However, my journey has unfolded just as it was intended to. My search for understanding and further spiritual awareness unfolded according to my readiness and according to the divine guidance of my life's journey.

Parenthood has been a huge growth experience. There is no dividing line between the lessons of my spiritual life and those within my lovely and forever-challenging family. Reflecting on the whole of my life experiences in this writing presents a bird's-eye view of a fast-moving and meaningful movie, where the main character sighs deeply at the end, feeling a deep love and gratitude for all that is, including a deep and joyful spiritual consciousness. Chaos, heartbreak, and all, it is one awesome journey!

Our home has always been a place with lots of activity. Physical energy has always been in abundance. For me, physical energy is enhanced and elevated by the energies of my spiritual path. The duality of physical and spiritual energies has dissolved into a balanced system. Gaining an awareness of my energy system has become a part of my daily spiritual practice. Life is so much easier when I can recognize and quickly call my spirit back from negative thoughts and environments. The reflections presented here flow out of chakra energy center one through chakra level five (will power) experiences, not necessarily in any particular order.

In summary, I have returned to my youthful state of mind—living in discovery with total acceptance. Life is going to be different every day. Nothing remains the same. Change is forever constant! To *l-i-v-e* is to move forward through the new, the ambiguous, always with a faith in life that all is well, sustaining strength through God's grace, and a deep and infinite gratitude for all that is. I know firsthand that letting go of the old makes room for the new, whether I am cleaning out the closet or cleaning out my life. In gaining education and knowledge toward something new, something you love doing, the spirit always supports and moves with you.

God is Creator, and we are most like God when we are creating. Humility, passion, compassion, forgiveness, appreciation, and loving energy—these are our "access codes," along with the *Essential Code*—that integrates our humanness with the divine. The Code and our co-creative synergy in communion and unity with others is how we seed and sustain the necessary changes in the new world age.

My perceptions are still transcending; the upper chakra experiences are still in progress, still unfolding. I find higher evolved spiritual consciousness difficult to explain, as are all inner experiences of the spirit. Words are inadequate, and the experiences are beyond emotion; just pure, divine love in an evolving, infinite, and illuminating light of discovery. Being an old soul (versus a baby, young, or mature soul), I find contentment, joy, and gratitude in all that is beautiful and serene. I see beauty in all of life. Even though the deep inner paths of the upper chakra experiences are not an easy thing to explore, Part VI of this book delves into these experiences.

Consider taking a personal inventory. Who are you? Where are you in reference to what has been presented here? I do this frequently. It's a very helpful exercise. Meditation, spending some time in total silence and solitude, is recommended. It is in silence that we meet God. Everything we learn, we learn for God and return home with our gifts of knowledge and advancement of our soul.

♥ Further insight at *www.TheEssentialCode.com* ♥

Existing Enigmas Of Cosmology

Inserting a bit of cosmology with the chakras: *nothing goes backward;* everything evolves, spiraling onward and outward, just like the spirit. Stagnation brings decay, a universal principle that applies to everything. The chemicals and conditions that allowed for this moment to be will never be *exactly* the same again. Everything changes—continually moving onward. Cosmology is the *universe as a whole,* which includes the living organism Earth and all life. We are a part of the whole: a particle or participant in the whole of all that exists—an interconnected energy. The universe continually expands outward by the evolving consciousness of mankind. As above, so it is below.

Since there is no backward movement in real time, isn't it obvious that we cannot exactly recreate what was? Try to instill this into the psyche of a status quo, or a woundology group! They may understand the reasoning but would be in denial that it applies to the self or their group. Control issues become embedded—an impulsive need to control everyone and everything; they trust only those in their group. Their defense messages are those involving blame, shame, and "poor me" terminology. They do not form new relationships; they take *"hostages."* Hostages have a right not to participate in either active or passive crazy-making. They can walk away anytime, put their energies to better use, and continue on the evolving journey of their spirit-self.

Apply this to a marriage situation where one leaves, seeking change for whatever reason. In dysfunctional groups, there will often be one family member or more who will try to keep the family gatherings the way they have always been. If the culture runs deep, you will find that they often do not graciously accept anyone new into the family. It gets tricky, but unfortunately it happens!

Leaving a relationship is often seen as a betrayal. When this happens, look closely to discern if it may actually be divine intervention for letting go of an old way of being and discovering the new—an awareness opening experience, in which one moves out of a stagnating circumstance in discovery of the self, igniting necessary and evolving new growth. When family members or whole family structures stagnate, it often creates division. These are riddles of cosmology that happen in the journey to the heart; a journey that takes one into the heart chakra, where one learns to effectively resolve life's issues and experience the necessary transitions to self-awareness and greater understanding of the human spirit. Our passage through the heart is one that heals and moves beyond issues of the first three chakras, evolving into the love and essence of unifying energies.

PART VI

Cultivating the Soul

*"You cannot be a spiritually evolved person and an
emotionally un-evolved person at the same time."*
—Gary Zukav, Soul to Soul, 2007

Valley of Sorrow, Evolutions of Light

My daughter-in-law rang our doorbell at seven in the
morning one day. I assumed she was going to the special
market a few blocks away to get supplies for a weekend cookout.
We went to the kitchen and waited for my husband to join us.
*I went numb in disbelief and horror as we were told that our youngest
son had committed suicide during the night.* I hope never to relive
the pain that we both felt! He was thirty-one years old; he had
always been concerned, caring, and attentive to us. A tall man
with wide shoulders and great strength, a teddy bear of warmth,
he was the first one to respond when others needed help. Oh,
dear God, there is no greater pain than the loss of one's child.

I moved like a robot for the next few weeks, going through
the motions of what had to be done. I immediately poured
myself into studies of the afterlife. I *had* to know! I *had* to
understand! Our son had left loving letters for us, as well as
instructions for his belongings and directions for his cremation.
He wished for his ashes to be spread in the most beautiful
areas in the western part of our state, where tall hills and deep
terrains filled one's eye with God's creations. Reading this, I
suddenly regretted that I never had the opportunity to take

him to my home state of Colorado to view the beautiful Rocky Mountains. I was deeply saddened by the things we didn't do that would have deeply touched his soul.

I went back to work at the family business two weeks after his death. I had to keep my mind busy. The studies I pursued led me to seek a top-notch medium as a means of healing and to possibly contact our son.

Through James Van Praag's online site, I found a well-recommended medium who had been a policeman in our area. And yes! Our son was waiting to speak! Communications with our son and conversations with the medium, as well as new insights into death and understandings of life on the other side of the veil helped me to survive and to heal from the deepest pain I have ever endured.

The whole experience delivered a quantum leap into the spiritual world; an illuminating light, a height and depth beyond anything I can explain. Our son has shared so much and has made his presence known in frequent and various ways. Our mutual love and connection to each other still run deep. I feel a strong, soul-to-soul, ever-present bond.

Masters, who inform us about life on the other side of the veil, explain that our soul continues to grow when we are on the other side, but at a slower pace than when here on the earth plane. Experiences on earth help us to resolve issues of the heart chakra and move into greater spiritual consciousness, enabling a more rapid advancement of our soul. This means that when we are developing, experiencing, healing, and evolving through the issues of our tribal zone, our addictions, beliefs, and wounds, with each transition/transformation/transcendence, we are actually doing our soul work! An unconscious, gravity-free cultivation of our soul!

All the pain, progressive healings, releasing of sacral vengeance, and blame games, all the negatives of our ego and emotions—these are all aspects of the transitions and transcendence required for a turning of the heart. Stop and think for a moment. How can one advance in conscious spirituality while still holding on to the feelings and ego traps of separateness, division, or vengefulness? One cannot get even or hold on to repressed anger and need for emotional turmoil and still evolve in the spirit at the same time! It's not even logical.

One cannot migrate through the heart chakra clinging to sacral energies. Instead, one can become stuck, unable to evolve to experience the sacred and elevated energies within the upper chakras (becoming one with the spirit). Our efforts in forgiveness, healing, acceptance, and growing are the nurturance that cultivates our soul. It is not a pain-free journey. Life on earth is not a pain-free experience. Pain is a symptom, indicating that something new is required: forgiveness, surrender, and a turning of the heart. One will need to cultivate a deep trust in life before initiating change and new life energies, regardless of the type of pathology that has evolved.

To grow in the spirit is to seek the grace of understanding and wisdom. Release, surrender your will to God's will. You will know in your heart exactly what your challenge is. Courage and emotional stamina will enable you to transition and transform your energy through self-understanding, the seeking and sharing of knowledge, the forgiveness of self and others, and by turning of the heart to incarnate the *Essential Code.* Do whatever it takes to heal and advance, so your frequency vibration will soar to a new level of spiritual connectivity.

Relationships are our greatest challenges and our greatest teachers. No one goes through life as an island, with no emotion or interaction with others. It is easy to get along with those who think like we do. But our challenge is to interact with all that life presents, not only accepting the differences, but embracing them as beauty within each person. God did not create junk. We are created different from every other person. Everyone has lessons to be learned, talents to be given, and a mind, body, and soul to cultivate. Our task is not to dwell on the faults of others but to find and harvest our own weaknesses and strengths. It sounds easy enough, but it's not that easy to harness that kind of power. God didn't make the journey easy, because our purpose on Earth is to cultivate our souls with love, empathy, and compassion for self and others. We are here to co-create and to achieve oneness with God. No one is perfect; everyone's shadow side comes out from time to time. Make amends, ask forgiveness, and move on.

My heart has not only been broken, it's been torn wide open. Every experience of pain has moved me forward toward my destiny. The profound cultivation of our soul continues throughout our lifetime. My most painful experiences have flowed out of different developmental issues as I traveled the chosen paths of my life's journey. Many of these experiences began somewhat mildly and then became excruciating as my life unfolded.

I have experienced the usual amount of growing pains. One of the highlights of this earthly journey was the diagnosis of bipolar disorder in our youngest daughter. She was living in Africa when it became obvious, and one year later in Europe, she was diagnosed. Being so far away from each other was difficult. It was her strength, intelligence, and innate ability to understand her illness that enabled her to learn how to manage her condition. She was a psychology minor in college. I am gloriously and deeply thankful for her gift of insight! Still, it is not an easy life for her.

Through counseling and expert medical care, she has healed her teenage wounds and gained wisdom, insight, and a sharp reasoning ability. She is now applying her college degree as the head of an English department. She paces herself to avoid creating unnecessary stresses, and remains in counseling and monthly medical care. God's graces have blessed her and soothed our souls!

Interludes and Reflections

Along with the usual family struggles, I have had to deal with continuous opposition for as long as I can remember. Difficult experiences that evolved out of raising two children who were not mine, and the cultural and developmental differences that I encountered as a result, have helped me to grow intellectually, spiritually, and emotionally.

Transcending issues with control, recovery, and my own ego took me into midlife. My life was always intense, always challenged. In my fifties, a revelation hit my consciousness: I have never fit the "average" label in any context. Our children had grown and were living out their lives in their own individual ways. All was well, but I had hit a two-year stage of limbo. I felt that there had to be something *more,* spiritually. I pondered this at times, but didn't really seek to truly understand what it might be or worry about where to even look. This was the time just prior to our youngest son experiencing a deep heartbreak as a relationship came to an end. He was moving out of the home that he and his former fiancée had moved into just six months earlier.

The heartache of finding that she now "wanted her space" was devastating. I was heartbroken too. He had a restless life up until he fell in love. It seemed to be a mutual love between them. He had been the happiest and most contented that I had ever seen him. He loved their new home and was driven to make it the most beautiful he could. His handyman talents, coupled with her decorating skills, made it an adorable home. Breaking up was a complete and overwhelming surprise to him. He was the one who had to leave and try to find an apartment.

His personal belongings were packed for him and placed in his work warehouse, and he moved in with his sister.

Just one month later, we received the horrifying news of his suicide. I could write a book on just this experience alone. There are no words to adequately explain the closeness with God, the relationship with our son on the other side, and his acknowledgments of happenings on this side. I have read that, after several reincarnations in one of our earthly lives, we will experience the unnatural loss of a dear one. We will all eventually have the experience of not just having our heart broken, but broken wide open. I can't help but think that our son became the sacrificial lamb in this, and that he was living God's chosen life for this experience. I walk a different walk. I live in serenity and peace. I am in my son's company at all times. He is such a funny guy, a loving guy, and a highly spiritual guy as well. I know that life does not end; it just changes. I live my life as usual, but with an inner awareness that cannot be explained. My spiritual consciousness took a quantum leap!

With the passing of their youngest sibling, our family split up. Two went to therapy to heal. His brother did very well; he pursued every avenue until he could go on in peace and deep understanding. His sister quit therapy when there were no longer any words between her and the therapist. Actually, it was a time to search deep within as she didn't overcome her woundology from childhood. As the middle child, she harbors her pain to the point of ongoing, distant and silent vengeance.

The emotional pain of a split family was another hurdle to overcome. In my own healing, I wasn't able to reach them; they had no apparent interest in healing and seeking a holistic balance. I leave all of this in God's hands. What their journey consists of is beyond my knowing. I love them, and I am here for them all at all times. There is no indication of a pursuit to heal and move on. For some, it is easier to remain in their wounds than to grow; our two lovely daughters live separate lives.

Transcending the emotional pain of a divided family was not easy, but it was easier than enduring the pain from the loss of our son. It begins with surrendering expectations. I can't expect my family to be a certain way, let alone the ideal way. Acceptance is the next step; I must learn to forgive and accept them all—just as they are—with unconditional love. I have learned to let go and let be. Only God knows what is to be. I have surrendered everything that's out of my control to the universe. We continuously send them love and blessings for their health and happiness, in the knowledge that God's intended journey for them is unknown, as is ours.

We enjoy family times with our sons and our youngest daughter and family. Everyone is so very good to us. We are truly blessed! Accepting imperfections in life challenges our spirit and initiates our souls' growth. Success in life is accepting *what is* with love and deep gratitude, while continually seeking to know God more dearly and more clearly through a deep, conscious and evolving awareness.

This journey has not been boring. Every single day, I look forward to an ongoing discovery of the new. I evolve by choice, rather than by chance. The journey through life grows lighter with each joyous transition and birthing of new vibrations of being and living. I am in love with life and all that it offers. I feel this deep within each morning as my senses come alive with joyful giddiness, realizing there is another day ahead of me to fill until it spills over into the night. How privileged can one be?

Have You Ever Thought about Life as a Continuing Journey of Cycles?

Treasured cycles of joy and happiness . . . of surrender and unfulfilled desires . . . of the pain and agony of loss . . . of forgiveness and transition . . . of an acceptance that is filled with an abundance of love and gratitude for what is: these are cycles of blissful contentment nestled within a deep spiritual consciousness. But always, this subtle tranquility relents to another cycle and another challenge. This is not unlike the patterns of the universe, where small cycles of cosmic events evolve within larger ones. This is the way with all that exists! Small cycles evolve within larger cycles, a reflective mirror of our multidimensional being. Try thinking of it as a mirrored, holographic ball where each little particle/mirror reflects a part of who you are.

*As above, it is below . . . t*he universe, too, is like a holographic ball with each small *particle* reflecting the whole. John Wheeler stated in 1998, "**We live in a 'participatory' universe not already created and we plop down in it. The world is a reflection; we are particles of the universe, creating it as we go, through our inner being'.**" John Wheeler's research was shaking the foundation of how our world works. The masters have given us powerful resources in scientific and spiritual intelligence that, once assimilated, enlighten our path toward a quantum state of spiritual consciousness. At the beginning of life, with our beginning minds, we experience *external conflict*. As we evolve, our minds become empowered and we experience events of *inner conflict*, still through our personal or beginning mind. In developing, healing, and experiencing the necessary movement *through* our heart chakra, we unfold into an open mind. An open mind is able to discern and accept new ways of thinking and being. It is able to unfold and transform, so that we can give our lives over to God and evolve into the impersonal mind, where we *learn without conflict.*

Pioneering research with profound insights is a precious gift for those seeking self-empowerment and holistic insight. It is crucial for those looking for the ability to perceive the connectivity among all beings, the universe and how it works, the cosmic soul, energy and spirit verses concreteness; the world (with all life and life experience), and how we are wired into the "whole." When we truly give our life to God, we accept our human responsibility to evolve as caring and passionate servants of all God's creation and divine intelligence, an unlimited and creative source.

In comparison, how shallow is the self-focused faith and dogmas of our day? The infinity of creation demands infinitude of holistic-based and feeling prayer response, which evokes both heart and emotion. From there, we become filled to the brim with gratitude for the awesomeness of our spirit life's journey in the human experience.

As our soul's journey evolves into the higher frequency levels of energy (elevations in the upper chakras), the time and space that it takes for daily challenges to evolve through our energy system will become shorter and shorter. Our task is to seek the path of divine guidance and nurturance and self-development and empowerment, always with unwavering discernment. We must choose that which emanates the inspiring and elevated energies of the divine. Once one passes through the heart chakra, one's insight and knowledge resonates with the higher frequencies of the upper chakras.

Elevated spiritual transitions of the sixth chakra energy field can be experienced when one resolves and heals emotional wounds, a transcendence from the negative energies and emotional aspects of the tribal mind, and the powers of the first three chakras. One must have a shifting of the ego and have transitioned through the systematic process of the fourth chakra. Thus, you can experience the essence of selfless love, embedded in faith and reliance on God's will (versus self-will). When one surrenders self-will and trusts in God's will, one transcends fear itself. Enabling clarity and intuitive insights of the third eye, a sixth sense discernment of truth, allows one *to see as spirit* (versus limitations of the rational mind). The energy of this chakra invites the essential self to one's full spiritual potential, fostering oneness with God and evolving in evolutionary consciousness and levels of the whole being—all that one has been (the past), all that one is (the present), and all that one can be (the future). Spiritual potential manifests through an open mind that seeks new wisdom by evolving in consciousness and universal intelligence, and going beyond illusions, elements, and senses. With that comes the total transcendence of the mundane.

In the discernment of truth, one comes to understand that everything is connected to everything else. Our earth and the universe is interconnected in one bio-system and that the universe is a seamless web that interconnects, holding within it all that is. There is an inter-connectivity between humanity and the stars, the earth and rocks, and water and plant life. Consider the scientific theory that we are made of stardust. We share the same chemicals as the stars, earth, rocks, water, and plants. That the 30/70 percent solid matter/water runs true in the biochemistry, etc.

How does one experience evolutionary consciousness? It's a source and creation, a deep, caring awareness of Earth, the universe, the co-creative process of nature, and the 14 billion-year story of creation: with a third-eye vision of humanity's place within the ages and epochs of man's earthly journey, *seeing* the whole evolutionary story with greater keenness than an eagle's eye.

The 'third eye' carries the vision and awareness that we exist on all levels simultaneously. That what we do and who we are incarnates into one's psyche and into the body of one's mundane life, affecting all levels of one's being. We exist in the past, the present, and the future. When one transitions into a new and elevated spirit of being, one also advances the soul, sending a trickling effect of this timeless energy into all of the earth and all life, which ripples into the cosmos.

We are spiritual beings having human experiences, *growing our souls*. Human DNA is imprinted with Hebrew letters meaning "God eternal within" (according to Gregg Braden,

The God Code, Hay House, 2005, www.greggbraden.com); our DNA can be changed by evolutionary, elevated developmental process through heartfelt transitions into oneness with growth in consciousness (according to Barbara Marx Hubbard, *Visions of a Universal Humanity*, www.barbaramarxhubbard.com). *So it is*, everything is interconnected (according to Thomas Berry, *The Dream of The Earth*, 1988, and Brian Swimme, *Brian Swimme and The Canticles to the Cosmos*, www.brianswimme.org). In the sixth chakra energy, we become detached from perceptions and see the truth, the symbolic meaning in situations. Detachment as a practice means fulfilling responsibility and accountability, and then surrendering the results to God's will. We do what we can, then let go of the outcome in trust.

Seventh chakra energy is where knowingness resides; the spirit knows things beyond what the mind knows. This is the crown chakra; energy from the supreme consciousness enters at this energy point and vibrates to all energy centers (chakras), and grounds us to the earth. The dark night of the soul appears, calling one to devoted prayer and daily spiritual practice.

A deep and awesome love embraces the reality that all is *one*—source . . . universe . . . earth . . . life . . . and all of creation—interwoven whole. Many find it difficult to wrap their minds around this universal truth. But with awareness of the spirit and the God within, coupled with a deep and profound consciousness, ***"All is one" is a simple, sacred, and powerful truth that resonates within the soul***. A wondrous awe can be found when initiating one's heartfelt commitments to do whatever it takes and to assure that the delicate balance and boundless beauty of all creation remains an infinite and sacred whole.

Wholeness is sustained by the active passion, heart-filled love, compassion, resonance, and peace of universal humans, co-creating with others to heal the living organism we know as planet Earth. ***The greatest challenge ever, in all of man's recorded*** *history, is already here: birthing an emerging embryo, a new world age, and co-creating new, sustainable global systems that resonate with heart energy—the sacred essence of the Essential Code!*

The Essential Code

What is it? The *Oxford American Dictionary* defines essential as "indispensable" and "of/or constituting a thing's essence." The deductive meaning therefore could be interpreted as the ***"indispensable essence of a thing."*** The thing we are relating to here is the *code*. So the question becomes, "How does one *crack the code?"* Code can be associated with a secret or it can be associated with a pre-arranged set of words representing a message.

Simple words that we hear frequently tend to float through one's psyche and mental digestive and comprehensive processes, lacking any memorable impressions. Simple words become so commonplace that they tend to lose value and are mentally tossed aside as already known. The familiarity and simplicity of the words become a matter of indifference and inertia. Especially when the words are at cross purposes to aloof, dormant feelings; where the meanings are so readily available to the brain that they are passively taken for granted because we feel we are totally aware of their meaning. When in fact, compelling belief is missing, so is applied action regarding the vital importance for an alert and profound response. And most of all, the heart-resonating urgency required. In the *Essential Code, the vital feelings are embedded into **one** identifiable phrase.* Seeing and hearing *the Essential Code, one* will be alerted to the *love* content of the *code and its loving urgency!* Because this code holds an *indispensable essence in a set of divine, pre-arranged words, the Essential Code* becomes sacred, not secret!

Secrecy is a dysfunctional trait in human behavior patterns. A non-resonating trait in universal energies of unity and oneness.

Building a New Wisdom

The Founding Fathers of America were sacred earthly vessels, the trailblazers who founded a nation under God! They were living out their humanness while ambitiously fulfilling their purpose here in the Earth School. The US Constitution was not founded on dogmas of religion, but on natural law. We are spiritual people by nature. Nature is declared a natural process of cellular creation. A cell is life. Cells are free entities, valued for their differentiation and evolutionary potential in a cosmic (divine) environment that encompasses and equates all humanity. *Every human being has inherited the cosmic right to the spontaneous evolution of life, responsible liberty, and the sacred pursuit of happiness.*

To evolve means to develop into different forms. The human potential develops, by nature, into different forms of being and into deeper, greater consciousness. Religion has the tendency to keep things as they have always been. We need to go beyond dogmas to grow in spiritual consciousness. As Abraham Lincoln stated, "Dogmas of the past do not apply to the future." **A missing element in society is a unified, global understanding of what spiritual growth really is.** The following informative statement clarifies the confusion of this "inside job" (inner journey in awareness and psycho/spiritual development):

If spiritual work does anything, it challenges and disturbs with just as much force and surprise as it illuminates and enlightens. In fact, if our spiritual work does not challenge what we know, if it does not disturb our habitual patterns of thought, perception, and action, then, it is not spiritual work at all; it is merely a form of self-medication."

~ ROBERT RABBIN, CONTEMPORARY MYSTIC AND FOUNDER OF RADICAL SAGES (WWW.RADICALSAGES.COM).

As Victor Frankl stated, when we are no longer "able to change a situation, we are challenged to change ourselves." (*Man's Search for Meaning, 1946*) We cannot change what is happening in the epochs of time. A new world age is birthing a new cosmic destiny. Its timing is precisely set according to divine plan and requires new insights, new wisdom, and a sixth sense capable of seeing the new world age as an embryo birthing into being. This will be a newborn age in need of nurturance, synergies of love, compassion, gratitude, and appreciation. The energies of the emerging new world age differ from that of the familiar world we now have engrained in our psyche. Our challenge is to match the new energy vibrations, spiritual vibrations of divine energies challenging humanity to co-create the kind of world we previously only dreamed of. As one shifts to new levels of understanding and harmony, the universe unconditionally supports the co—creative process of unity, a synergy of heart-based and co-active communities in communion.

The heart is the organ that energetically connects to the electromagnetic waves of the universe. As Gregg Braden says, *"In addition to pumping the blood of life within our bodies, we may think of the heart as a belief-to-matter translator. It converts the perceptions of our experiences, beliefs, and imagination into the coded language of waves that communicate with the world beyond our bodies."*

The energies and conditions now present in the universe, and their effect on extremes in weather, are too complex for our politicians and local media experts to explain. This is also true of new knowledge regarding our human potential to influence global activity through human emotions and heartfelt feelings (energy). How can human emotions of love and compassion connect with divine energies of the universe to affect desirable outcomes? When a collective mass of loving energy flows into an atmosphere of loving essence and light (energy), this influx of energy influences and nurtures the vibration level of the whole.

With the above knowledge, can you now understand why the energies of love, gratitude, and compassion are energies to embody in our hearts? If it isn't a heartfelt emotion, then it's not a conducive energy. HeartMath Science has calculated that the heart-quality of a small percentage of the global populace can make a huge difference. (A viable number to make that difference is the energy of one hundred people out of a million.) The universe is a blanket of wise and intelligent energy. We strengthen and co-create with that energy by activating the *Essential Code.*

The Essential Code incarnates a transcended ego with deep feelings of peace, love, forgiveness, appreciation, gratitude, and compassion. Then, bonding this indispensable essence within one's heart as one's sacred way of being and living. Swift embodiment of this sacred way of being, and co-creating new systems in community and unity, is an urgency of all time!

We must be what we want the world to be. We must work together to create *communities in communion, co-creative cells that nurture the earth and all creation, and above all, a unity where all is* **one,** *requiring an active, alive, Essential Code at the core of our communities and evolutionary souls.* **The effectiveness of this synergy process is a scientifically proven reality** (Heart Math Institute monitoring device).

The Global Coherence Initiative Project has a Care link on their website, where more than twenty-one thousand people (at press time) from eighty countries participated in directing heartfelt love and compassion toward troubled areas around the globe. They have proven that when this energy is simultaneously and collectively directed, it effectively quiets the turmoil and even violence. *(Ref: Gregg Braden, Fractal Time, Hay House, 2009)* Get on board! Participate in manifesting this new species in human evolution!

Remember John Wheeler's statement at the beginning of this chapter? "We live in a *participatory* universe, the world is a reflection, we are particles of the universe, *creating it as we go, through our inner being!*" Open the mind, learn without conflict, and see the awesomeness of who you are. You are a particle, participating in the whole of creation with every loving feeling you generate! Quantum cosmology is here, now. It's flowing, spiritual consciousness cultivating our soul into a oneness with all that is. It's an illuminating *awe!* Will you participate? Align with new wisdom and master your spirit by mastering the Essential Code! Create a meaningful impact now and beyond your wildest dreams of the future!

The continuity of my mission on Earth requires ongoing evolution of my soul, with a clear and open door for God's eternal love, which counteracts the fragmented negativity of unawakened souls. My personal goals are to experience ongoing systemic development in co—creative, evolutionary consciousness and to eternally learn, educate, and co-create in communion.

The *Essential Code* is an *urgent* challenge, one that will always be urgent for all of humanity. The *Essential Code* is imperative in birthing of the new world age and nurturing this new embryo. This is man's new way of being, the path to an infinite and sacred destiny. It's an urgency of the heart!

~ Love, *gratitude, compassion, co-creative synergy,*
peace, appreciation, and cooperation ~

"Cosmic Consciousness"

You Are Source Energy!
♥ Further messages at *www.TheEssentialCode.com.* ♥

At The Mid-Life Journey
Arvetta M. Souza (at age 54)

"When we understand us, our consciousness,
we also understand the universe and the
separation disappears."
- Amit Goswami, physicist -

APPENDIX A
TYPICAL COMMENTS

Typical Comments: KOHLBERG STAGES. APPENDIX A – (unknown source)

Level: PRE-CONVENTIONAL

Stage	Obligation	Punishment	Property Rights	Value of Life
1. Obedience - punishment orientation	I'm going to school today because if I done I'll get spanked.	He broke the, so to stay out of jail he'd better get the best lawyer he can	These are my marbles and I'm going to keep them until somebody takes them from me.	You should save a drowning man because he might be important or have a lot of money.
2. Personal interest orientation	I'm going to school today because I'll get an "A" on the spelling test.	He broke the law, but maybe he can work out a deal with the lawyer and judge so he get's off with a lighter sentence.	These are my marbles, buy I will give you three of them for a bite of your hot dog.	You should save a drowning man because he might give you a reward for doing it.

Level: CONVENTIONAL

Stage	Obligation	Punishment	Property Rights	Value of Life
3. Good-boy, good-girl orientation	I keep going to school because all my friends are there and my parents expect me to go.	He broke the law, but since his intentions were good they should give him a light sentence.	This is my land, and I'm going to build a house that will go nicely with the other houses in the community.	You should save a drowning man because his family will appreciate it and your friends will congratulate you for doing it.
4. Authority and social-order - maintaining orientation	I am going to school because the law says I have to go until I'm sixteen.	He broke the law, so he must be punished to full extent of the law.	This is my house - I worked hard to get it, and I deserve to keep it.	You must try to save a drowning man because the law requires you to give help to people in distress.

Level: POST-CONVENTIONAL

Stage	Obligation	Punishment	Property Rights	Value for Life
5. Social Contract orientation	I'm going to college because I feel I should become a lawyer and work within the system to improve our society.	He broke the law, so he should be sent to jail until he changes his ways and becomes a law-abiding citizen.	This is my business, if the town council tells me that its cooperation is affecting the environment in this community,'I'll take care of the problem.	You should try to save a drowning man because it's important that everyone in our society be concerned about the welfare of others.
6. Conscience orientation	I'm going to college because I feel I should become a social worker & help others to climb out of the poverty and ignorance in which they live	He broke the law, but if we can find out why he did it, maybe we can get rid of his problem without throwing him into jail and turning out another hardened criminal.	This is my factory, but if I find that its operation is harming individuals by polluting the environment, I'll correct the problem immediately, even if it means closing.	You should try to save a drowning man because every individual human life is important and is worthy of respect and protection.

APPENDIX B
MASTERY

"Mastery is not about perfection, but practicing it; like a moving star, we can use our 'guiding star' to move toward our potential. We often veer off and dabble in another way . . . the obsessive! We eventually discover we were right the first time out!

"Mastery means diligently, patiently, persistently, playfully, goal setting. Goal setting without action is a pattern for failure. Mastery is to love it so much that for every mile we take toward our goal, we hope the destination was further away! Work hard, don't be lazy.

"In Mastery there are endless climaxes—like in the movies or media—with no plateau We have to get into the plateau to love it! We make life a practice, now. Meditating everyday!

"The question is: What are our practices? Consistency on the fundamentals is the hallmark of success. Remembering that we have a 'homo' status point (genius) —recognize that; you can continue to push beyond a 'normal' state. Honor it!"

~ GEORGE LEONARD

REFERENCES

The author gratefully wishes to acknowledge and recommend the following resources:

Arjuna Ardagh, *Awakening Into Oneness,* Sounds True Publications. www.soundstrue.com, 2007.

Thomas Berry, *The Dream of the Earth, Sierra Club,* 1988.

Gregg Braden, *Fractal Time, the Secret to 2012 and the New World Age.* Hay House, *2010.*

Gregg Braden, *The Divine Matrix.* Hay House, 2007.

Gregg Braden, *The Isaiah Effect.* Three Rivers Press, 2001.

Gregg Braden, *The God Code.* Hay House, 2004.

John Bradshaw, *The Family, A Revolutionary Way of Self-Discovery.* Health Communications, 1988.

John Bradshaw, *Homecoming: Reclaiming and Championing Your Inner Child.* Bantam Books, 1990.

John Bradshaw, all CD and video programs (Too numerous; reader choose: www.johnbradshaw.com).

Wayne Dyer, *Change Your Thoughts, Change Your Life.* Hay House, 2007.

Dennis Edwards, theological consultant, *Made from Star Dust.* Collins Dove, 1992.

Erik H. Erikson, *The Life Cycle Completed,* by Joan Erikson. W. W. Norton, 1997.

James Fowler, *Stages of Faith Development, the Psychology of Human Development & the Quest for Meaning, Harper & Collins Publishers, 1981-1995*

Barbara Marx Hubbard, *Visions of a Universal Humanity* (video), www.barbaramarxhubbard.com.

Lawrence Kohlberg, *Kohlberg Stages of Moral Development,* 1958 from *Wikipedia.org.*

Hans Küng, *The Catholic Church, A Short History.* Modern Library (www.modernlibrary.com), 2003.

Caroline Myss, *Why People Don't Heal and How They Can.* Harmony Books, 1997.

Caroline Myss, *Anatomy of the Spirit.* Random House (www.randomhouse.com), 1996.

Brian Swimme, *Canticle to the Cosmos.* Center for the Study of the Universe (www.brianswimme.org).

Janet Woititz, *Adult Children of Alcoholics.* Health Communications, 1990.

ABOUT ARVETTA

Arvetta was born on the eastern flats of Colorado, moving to Denver at age seven. Following her education and marriage, she moved to the east coast of Massachusetts, settling in Malden, a suburb of Boston. She has a large grown family and assisted in the family business while following her deep desire for learning and spiritual evolution. She achieved seven years education in the humanities, two years in business, and lifetime studies in various arenas of spirituality.

With more than twenty years in pastoral ministries, Arvetta transcended the limiting dogma of organized religion to a cosmic spirituality and evolutionary consciousness. She has been active in the Virtual Co-Creative Community (VCCC), an international, co-creative, social action group, virtually manifesting in a resonant field, mentored by Barbara Marx Hubbard.

The Essential Code – Feeling the Urgency of Your Heart is Arvetta's first book. She offers a different approach in spiritual awakening and enjoys assisting the transformative journey of others. She lives with her husband, Manny, and extends her love and an abundance of blessings to her family and friends, and to all pioneering souls co-creating our sacred destiny.

www.TheEssentialCode.com.